Confessions of a Sexist

Confessions of a Sexist

Lars Einar Engström

ATHENA PRESS
LONDON

ISBN 10-digit: 1 84748 114 0
ISBN 13-digit: 978 1 84748 114 6

First published in Swedish in 2005 by
Konsultförlaget
Uppsala Publishing House AB
Box 207, 759 02 Uppsala
Sweden

Published in Denmark in 2007 by
Aschehoug Dansk forlag A/S
Vognmagergade 11
1148 Copenhagen

Published in Iceland in 2007 by
Leshus Publishing
Bókhlödustígur 6B
101 Reykjavik
Iceland

Published 2008 by
ATHENA PRESS
Queen's House, 2 Holly Road
Twickenham TW1 4EG
United Kingdom

Printed for Athena Press

For:
Astrid and Einar

Thanks:
Gabriella Brandon-Cox for the translation
Jennyfer Brandon-Cox for the photo for the cover
And to my supporters: Greta, Jacob, Mats, Ahlm and Staffan.
A special thanks to Thomas Linquist at Linqsearch.

Contents

Introduction

Who Calls Himself a Sexist?

For the past twenty-five years I have taken an active part in the business world, both as a consultant running my own company and as personnel manager in the fields of entertainment and computers. For a number of years, I was responsible for the European managership development in an American computer company.

I have held hundreds of conferences within the fields of communication and leadership and have developed leadership programmes in cooperation with INSEAD in France and London Business School in the UK. I am a psychologist, and since 1992 I have run my own consultancy within the line of recruitment and organisation development. I have been part of about ten management groups and I have acted as adviser to many young people, men as well as women.

Once, in a conference in 2002, I raised the issue of equality.

Once, in twenty-five years.

While working on this book, I have read a great deal about women and their fight for equality and it has indeed worried me. Certainly, some progress has been made during the past hundred years, but not as much as is sometimes claimed. Not structurally, not profoundly.

What is sexism? According to the dictionary, sexism is a way of behaviour that means discrimination on the basis of gender. According to my own definition, it is when one of the sexes considers itself standing above the other. The result of that is the creation of an imbalance. This means that women can be sexists, too. I claim that I have met such women. And you probably have too.

Many Women Are Even Better

For sure, women are being heard and seen more today than ever before, but only if you look and listen really carefully. Unfortunately, there are still a substantial number of men who close their eyes and hope that the nightmare will disappear. The nightmare consists of the unpleasant fact that many women are just as capable, or even more so, in a wide range of fields. And I am not referring to domestic work, childcare or nursing. I have looked upon myself as a man with modern values. But I turned out to be wrong and it has taken me years to discover that. It also required some incidents beyond my control to make me see what it was really like. It was when I started to study the field of equality that my view of femininity, masculinity, feminism and equality gradually changed. Many are the occasions when I have discussed equality with female managers and tried to understand their situation. During the process of creating this book, I interviewed about thirty women in prominent posts within trade and industry.

I have also participated in a number of seminars on the subject and I have, as mentioned, read quite a number of books. And I have learnt a lot. The oppression is worse and more complex than I ever could have imagined.

The Picture Is Clear

Generally, the picture is rather distinct: there is superiority and there is inferiority and women come off worst. But despite this we act as if this subject has to be studied over and over again. I find that strange. We know that the men and the boys are those who need to broaden their vision. And yet we stubbornly seek more information to support this knowledge instead of dealing with the actual problem. But that is perhaps not so surprising. According to custom, women are the ones to adjust to current circumstances. Nowadays, voices are raised for the participation, changing and developing of men.

An important event in my own process of understanding was when I sat with my daughter Jennyfer, at that time seventeen years old, discussing her school, career and future. As usual,

Jennyfer thought I had strange ideas and a strange way of handling things. She looked at me and said: 'You know, Daddy, I have always thought that you have brain damage.'

And suddenly I realised that she meant it. She really meant that. Every word.

Hopefully, I have not got brain damage. But I have definitely been brainwashed and fooled, as have many of my brothers out there.

Nowadays I look upon the world with opened eyes, and when I use a woman's perspective on values and conduct I do not recognise myself. I have passively and actively participated in this oppression and I have defended the current order of discrimination on the basis of gender.

And to be honest, I am ashamed of myself. But only to a certain degree, as I do not consider the fault to be entirely mine – even though I am fully aware of that I alone carry the ultimate responsibility.

I was raised – well, drilled – to believe that men are better than women and therefore shall be in charge. Women tend the household and take care of the children and therefore ought to work part-time. Men take care of the economy and support the family. I am a Swedish, middle-aged, white man with my own consultancy business and I have made a career both nationally and internationally. I was the apple of my mother's eye and the one that lifted the status of the family from working class of Skutskar (all chimneys and smoke from the sulphate mill) to the crème de la crème of Paris.

I still consider men to be superior, even though I know it is wrong. I know that men and women have the same value. But the thought does not come naturally. The delusion is deeply rooted. My upbringing, advertising, TV and film have all affected my fifty-year-old brain and my way of thinking. But I have not given up. Intellectually, I know what is right and what is wrong, and I want to change. Even though I know that values run deep.

On the Side of Women

I am writing this book as a contribution to the debate surrounding equality and career. To avoid any misunderstanding, I want to emphasise that I am on women's side. I am a witness, ready to give evidence. It is time to confess.

Accusations given through the media are quite true but we men do not take these matters seriously. You could say that the sexists have changed strategy, which enables us to continue our segregation. Men claim to be in favour of equality and the principle of equal pay, but that is only as long as it does not affect their own sphere of influence and salary. To be politically correct, we are all officially on women's side. But that, of course, is not true. A majority, in which I include many supportive women, are in favour of the men and their rights.

To succeed in life you have to develop as a human being, which means to be content with who you are and what you have achieved. Many agree that career and money are secondary to true basic values.

But then there are some who do not: people carrying a lifelong deception, believing happiness comes with money and possessions. In their private thoughts these people, mostly men, arbour other points of view. By joining the patriarchy they hide their inferiority towards women, their dread of them and their fear of being left outside the fellowship.

But the patriarchy is rocking. Women are gradually let in, because we have no other options.

The Necessity of Generalising

Despite our individual and gender differences we are rather alike, so in order to draw conclusions, have discussions and analyse situations I need to generalise. And that is what I will do in this book.

A clear-cut example of a well-established generalisation relates to driving a car. As a driver I have to assume that other drivers I meet on the road are alert, concentrated and sober – otherwise I would not dare to get out there. But we know that is far from the truth. People drive affected with both alcohol and drugs, with screaming kids in the back seat and cellphones ringing.

If I did not accept my generalised picture of drivers I would have to spend an enormous amount of time and effort wondering about each and every driver I meet on the road and whether we are going to collide or not. Otherwise I would avoid going out in the traffic all together. So, as I said, this book is partly based on generalisations.

I am sure that some of you will raise objections. But I maintain that we often act and react in the same way, based on more or less conscious assumptions.

You might think that you are the exception that proves the rule, but I would like even you to consider my reasoning with an open mind. It is not until we are aware of our valuations and actions that we are able to make a change.

I start from a general picture of what I see and hear. Every day I see examples of men acting against women and I say that as a sex we are deceiving ourselves when we claim to be feminists and that we support equality. Men are all sexists, and I am one of them.

We put it in to our heads that we treat our fellow beings with dignity and respect and that we long for family life and responsibility. At the same time we regard ourselves as more valuable than women. We claim higher salaries, we offer a helping hand with the household, we babysit and we prefer to spend our time at work or keeping fit in some stadium than sharing it with our children. This is speaking with a split tongue.

Contribution to a Discussion or a Book about Management

Unfortunately, not only men are chauvinist pigs. Most people in our society are. I meet them in my everyday life – from Jacob, seventeen, to Annika, thirty-two, to Christer, fifty-seven, to Elsa, seventy-eight years old. This book aims to make manifest and confirm what most women already know: that men oppress women in a variety of fields, using obvious or hidden techniques. The book is also about company cultures, about how organisations handle matters of equality and leadership. And it is about what women who want to make a career need to consider in our unequal society. Hopefully, this book can be used to suggest debates within the field of leadership training in organisations and companies. Perhaps a few directors will find it useful as a source of inspiration. At the end of the book, I will introduce some plans of action and useful tools to use for anyone who is striving for changes.

Maybe this book also will work as an alarm clock to other sexists. I hope to reach men with power and influence who have started to reflect on their values and actions. Perhaps they can be awakened and become sensible sexists and from there start their progress to becoming more equal-minded in their way of thinking and acting. It is not until we are aware of our shortcomings that we can do something about them.

The Upbringing of a Sexist

The Upbringing and the Childhood

Retrospectively, I can see a clear pattern regarding my values in life. My mother was both strong and dominant. You may believe that these two words mean the same, but I think that there is an essential difference. In general, women are strong and men are dominant.

The strength of women is their unbending will to mix professional life with domestic life, to have another go with problems mounting up, to seek solutions and see opportunities. In short, women protect life.

Men's dominance is more artificial. Most men enjoy certain benefits just by being born men. We haven't earned the appreciation, but we get it from earliest infancy because we are boys. Young men dominate in the classrooms; boys and men get better practise hours in the sports arenas and more resources when it comes to leisure-time activities. The list is never-ending. My mother's upbringing turned me into a sexist. I did not fully realise this until I started to write this book.

However, she alone is not to blame. My father contributed as well as my grandfather and grandmother and the whole village where I grew up. Society in general carries the responsibility, not least my school. All my male friends are sexists and most of my female friends too.

Many men claim that they are feminists but those are just words. Our true values are deeply rooted. They cannot be changed overnight and it is a difficult procedure even over a longer period of time. Attitudes and behaviour are extremely difficult to change during a generation. You are brought up with certain values that you carry through life. My mother was literally a sexist and I became the same.

Good Girls, Bad Girls

I pictured and unfortunately still sometimes picture women as being one of two categories: the strong and the weak. The former, who were only a few, made careers and ruled with an iron hand. The latter you married in order to breed.

I may banter but I seriously claim that I had categorised men and women already in my early childhood. And the picture was either black or white. Good girls, bad girls, whores, madonnas, dragons and doormats. Even though I did not realise it then, I was brought up to be a sexist by a man and a woman who seemed to be normal and honest citizens. I still carry the good girl, bad girl syndrome with me and there is not a day when I don't try to handle it. I have made some progress but I know that I will never entirely get rid of that burden and that affects my everyday life.

Both my parents made sure that we children knew that women are not trustworthy. At the same time, my mother made us understand that we could put our trust in her, no matter what. Her motto was: 'Do what you like but don't come running to mummy when things go wrong.' It was not hard to choose then. You acted the way Mummy wanted for fear of being left alone.

The motto of my mother sounds like a threat, and a threat it was. Or, as the psychoanalyst Melanie Klein would have put it, conditional love. You bet it was effective! Even now, being an adult and eight years after my mother's death, I cannot help wondering if she would let me down if I were to defy her today. Deep down I think the threat was empty, but I never dared to challenge it.

Used in management, this method is just as effective. And I have met many leaders who have realised that. Men as well as women. Unfortunately, I turned into such a leader myself. Subconsciously guided by my mother, I have wondered around, furious if someone has 'let me down' and that behaviour has led to nothing but misery.

So, I do not trust women, why should I? Does anyone believe that you change your profound values and contradict Mummy just because someone suggests that? Not me, anyway.

Mother and Her Career

Mother raised us children and was in charge of the household. Father kind of symbolised working life and was responsible for punishments of more serious infringements. My mother was a housewife and did not start working outside home until I was eight years old. Then she started her career. So, unfortunately, I cannot blame my view of women on nursery school. That would have been comfortable, because that way I could have saved my mother's reputation.

But my attitude toward women comes from mother, my teachers in school, from film, media and from my father. In that order. Today, I realise that my father was in some ways a man with an open mind for equality. But he was unaware of that, and he was far ahead of his time. He did the cooking, baked, cleaned and he even went shopping. That was very unusual in Sweden in the 1950s. Somehow this has had an effect on me, but my mother's influence was far stronger. And we tend to follow the strongest, the most powerful. That is what I did and that is what all the men I have met have done. All?

My upbringing was not unique. You find the prejudices, the methods to create real men in all classes and on all levels in society. I guess that must be the only area where we all think alike, high or low.

Until my daughter was born in 1983, I looked upon myself as a man with a rather 'equal' basic view. But she has changed me in many ways, not the least regarding my attitude towards women. This came gradually, year by year, partly because I did not understand her – despite the fact that everybody said we were so alike – and partly because she had a strong will of her own. Actually, I am surprised every time I meet strong, rather independent women. I have grown accustomed to seeing them as dependent and I think I share that attitude with most men. Wherever I have met men – in school, in the army or at work – I have discovered that they all share my picture of girls as good or bad. So I never doubted my point of view. I was as indoctrinated as the rest.

At the same time I pictured myself on a higher level than my fellows, these male chauvinist pigs. At times I even felt sorry for them for not sharing my insights. It was like two worlds, one private and one public, and both were real. I could say that I did not care if we employed a man or a woman, but I never really meant it. And I did not see the paradox that my picture of men and women and their different roles in life was profoundly traditional.

The Awakening of a Sexist

I Had No Idea It Was This Bad

Although I have been surrounded by women for more than fifty years, I had no idea how bad the situation really was. How is that possible? Have I looked the other way, pretending not to see, or…?

There are several answers to these questions. They are linked together, and I will try to relate to you this whole problem, from my point of view.

In my world, women have always been a utility product. I may not daily have thought about women in those terms, but that has definitely been my fundamental principle. I grew up with that attitude and I still have it. I do not exaggerate when I claim that I have a daily battle with that.

I have joked about sex, been ironic, laughed along even at unfunny jokes. I have 'forgotten' female colleagues at lunchtime and so on. You know the old tricks. Harmless, I thought. But the women around me certainly did not agree.

Every day we have to face situations regarding equality, and it is hard to adjust to new ideas when you have played the game for over fifty years. I have spent most of my professional time in the business world, and I am not sure that I have done more good than harm. Many a time I have participated in excluding women with a broader competence than the male applicants. Actually, it is more frequent that I want to admit.

I have also neglected women who have been talking at meetings, regardless of the importance of their contributions. Sometimes, I have speculated with others as to whether or not a woman intended to have children or not in the near future, due to her being in a fertile age. The fact that there always are two persons involved in the process of pregnancy was something I never regarded.

I have, in short, been an arsehole.

Avoiding Listening

It has never occurred to me that not listening to women is to oppress. To me, it has always gone without saying that I as a man have the last word if that is what I want. If nothing else, that has made *my* life easier.

Of course I have been listening to women, but mostly out of courtesy. I have learnt how to look as if I am listening, in order to avoid trouble. When getting tired of all the babble, I have simply interrupted and put things right.

It is a lot easier to live if women are silent, and things run smoother if men – in other words I – take the decisions. Discussions last much longer if women are present. They also tend to be more complicated and emotional.

That is the way I have previously reasoned and I can see now how wrong I have been. It is a fact that it takes more time when emotions are involved or you are trying to make all participants in a group happy. Men are used to pointing out the direction like an officer, and anyone who is not with you is against you.

This is not a good strategy. It leads to nothing but conflict and a struggle for power. It is a male attitude and it is wrong.

Women Are Dropped

Women are often dropped just for being women, especially in managerial positions. I have consistently favoured men to women during my career as a recruiter. A man will not become pregnant, will not have periods and will not nurse children.

I do not even dare to think of how many women I have participated in stopping during twenty-five years of recruiting.

Any women with children are already doing a full-time job. Therefore, they are often excluded in the race for a position in a company. It is too expensive to appoint an unreliable manager who may not be there every day.

If a woman in a recruitment situation tells me that she and her husband share the domestic work and the nursing of the children, my client and I have glared at each other and afterwards said things like: 'What kind of sissy is she married to?' or 'She is obviously wearing the breeches. You wouldn't want to marry that one.'

That is what it can sound like in the business world of today. Not openly, of course, but behind closed doors. And sadly, it is not unusual.

However, there are movements against sexism – men who will not tolerate this way of thinking and women who dare to report the worst assaults. Especially within the academic world – many reports have been made there lately concerning sexist assaults. That is a healthy sign in an unhealthy society, and it brings hope for the future.

Who Is Responsible? The Female Oppression

Men have power and they oppress, we all know that. But I also believe that there exists a female oppression. For a number of years, women spend time with and dominate their children most of the day. The majority of children only spend time with their fathers during evenings and weekends. That shapes us and makes an impression.

The first ten to twelve years are the most important in our lives. That is when values are established. Most children attend nursery school and the junior and intermediate stages in comprehensive school during these years. There, they are mostly surrounded by women.

What happens there? Boys get attention and privileges that can only be connected to their sex. Boy/man – grab every opportunity. Girl/woman – wait for your turn. A boy gets a pat on his head when he is good or cocky. He is raised to be seen and heard. A girl gets a pat on her head for being quiet, modest, clean, neat and ambitious and for taking care of the boys. So there is no doubt that women are highly responsible for bringing up new little male chauvinists.

We must bring attention to our behaviour towards girls and boys. Honestly, we find a boy who can make himself heard in the sandpit rather refreshing, do we not? And we find a girl in a ballet outfit and a coiffure quite adorable.

During my entire upbringing, women dominated my life. Today I can state, and be rather upset about it, that under that cover of womanly kindness was hidden a huge amount of female oppression. After such a long period being told what to think, say, feel and do, I now enjoy the opportunity to make my own decisions. Sometimes I have a feeling of revenge about the whole thing.

As a boy, you long to be around men but wherever you look you see women. The men are absent, except for a few hours during weekends when they are around to teach you to be a man.

It is interesting that women raised me to be a sexist. And later in life, people in the male chauvinistic worlds of sports and arms added to that attitude. In the military service you learn that real men do not cry, that the lowest of the low are shrews and queer, that women should be fucked hard and gays sent off to Siberia in bundles. And I am not exaggerating – on the contrary.

When I grew up, I was told to be nice to girls. The word nice included a contempt for the weaker sex. Girls were vulnerable, could fall apart, and should be treated differently. This contempt only encouraged us boys to be more macho than necessary. We boys enjoyed privileges everywhere. We were allowed to be dirty, to arrive late and to raise our voices in the classroom. The girls had none of these privileges. They were supposed to be clean, neat and nice.

The difference in upbringing that I and my sister experienced, as well as the attitude towards us from society, has been significant. In school, I was one of the boys who bullied girls. But my friends and I did not see it that way; we really thought we were joking. Thinking back, I realise that I did not want to be part of the whole thing. I still sense a feeling of discomfort.

There's No Such Thing as Feminist Men

Women have asked me if I have also interviewed men regarding their responsibility concerning equality. The answer is yes and no. I have chosen not to study men because I don't find it necessary: partly because I am a man myself, partly because men do practically nothing at all when it comes to equality matters. It has always been like that.

Some men call themselves feminists and claim that they are helping women in various ways. I believe that is nonsense. These men are trying to benefit from something or are acting under pressure from the surroundings.

I think that I have never met a genuine male feminist. If they exist, I wonder where they are. It is not possible, as some men claim, to be a part-time feminist, in certain situations. What they mean by certain situations, I don't know.

One issue men often bring up is salary. Men often claim they are in favour of women having the same wages as men. 'When it comes to wages, I'm a feminist.' They can't be serious. Because if they are, how do they explain the actual differences in wages between men and women?

Men react in two ways towards women. We often pity them and try to be nice in order to give them a decent life. I'm not joking. Many men brag about their offering a helping hand in the domestic work and nursing the children so that their wives can have an evening off and go to see a movie with a friend, or maybe work overtime. A helping hand! With something that they are involved in together! This is everyday life for women in Sweden today.

I claim that men in general want women to shut up. We want them to listen, to be passive, obedient and service-minded. In short, to take care of us.

There exists a motive to hide this. Politicians as well as businessmen claim that we need more women in leading positions. Women, they declare, are just as competent as men.

But do men really believe that? During my twenty-five years in business, I have never met a man who deep down feels that way. Or one who has been really willing to speak in favour of hiring female managers. I haven't met one man willing to raise the question.

Many men know that it is beneficial for the group if you mix the sexes, but that is mainly a practical matter. And it sounds good to express the view.

Women in management rooms serve as mood raisers or fronts to the public. But their opinions don't count. It's not worth the effort to really listen.

Terrible Feminists

There is nothing men like better than to generalise and claim that feminists are ugly, lesbians and impossible to be around. The most effective way to handle opponents is to oppress them, bundle them together and put a label on them. This is what authorities have always done to maintain their power.

To be a woman is to be passive. That is good, something positive. Being a feminist is being active, and that's bad. Active women do what men do; they claim their rights and express themselves. They call matters in to question and are being questioned themselves. Obviously, men are threatened when women act the same way they do.

But what if there is a difference between feminists? What if not all of them are the same? The psychoanalyst Patricia Klein Frithiof, active at The Institute for Psychology of Women, describes feminism like this:

> Feminism is not a united theory. It consists of several different directions. Feminism is also an idea of the world, or several ideas of the world, including women and confirming the human dignity of women. Feminism is striving to visualise and analyse relations between the sexes (system of gender), power and all forms of oppression of women.

Harriet Goldhor Lerner, an American women's psychologist and therapist, represents a feminism that assumes that men and women are more like each other as human beings than we are different. Polarisations are destructive and alienate us instead of getting us closer to each other and teaching us something about human behaviour and togetherness. Lerner also suggests that women are not homogeneous as a group. The concept of women, as well as the concept of men, consists of a various number of individuals with a huge variety when it comes to acting and thinking. This is surely a new way of thinking, not the least for men. Most men see feminists as disturbing and beyond control and the rest as a group of ordinary women.

Screaming Women and Deaf Men

In my opinion, women are way too quiet. I am sure they talk to each other about their situation, but unfortunately not to men. We talk too little about these problems. No matter how much I try to find examples of demands for equality in my working life, I find nothing.

In the organisations where I have worked or have been in contact with, women have never demanded changes concerning appointments, strategies or structures in management or anything else that could be linked to equality. However, I have understood that many women feel that they loudly claim their rights and point at injustices. The problem seems to be that I and my male friends don't see or hear that. There is a communication problem somewhere along the road.

There are, of course, many reasons for this. I am not an expert at communications, but obviously we use different languages, different ways to handle situations, different techniques when it comes to arguing and different ways to express our views. I know men who are unable to hear a woman's story out since each man claims that he knows what she is going to say anyway. Men interrupt or fill in.

In private conversations I have had with women, issues of equality *have* been mentioned. Not often, but sometimes. Young women say, with a sigh, that they are treated this way because they are women. Older colleagues are even more resigned. 'This is the way it is, and has always been.' The issue has not reached further than that. No loud demonstrations, no sex refusal, no suffragettes.

I have on these occasions not known how to act or how to behave. I have no experience of my own in these matters and I haven't been trained to handle them either, so I have felt rather inadequate. Consequently, I have tried to change the subject or say something funny.

To Dare to Act

Any woman who feels oppressed should speak up at once. And, as a woman, she must dare to call things their names. 'I feel oppressed and run over. You insult me.'

Women must react and act together with the men who actually see and hear (they do exist even though they are often rather quiet). Debates held in the media are not enough. The issue must be thrashed out in everyday life, at the dinner table, during meetings, conferences and coffee breaks; here and now, everybody included. But the issue must be pursued by women. Men will not abdicate their position of power freely.

Examples from Everyday Life

Some time ago I had a meeting with a managing director and an information manager, both of them born in the sixties. These men shared the opinion that no women are willing to make a career for themselves.

'There might be a few capable, but where are the best?'

'There are many competent women,' I objected, deliberately avoiding the word capable.

I got some approval.

'Well, maybe, but most women don't want to be managers. They want to stay at home or work part-time.'

Some years ago I would have said something like that myself, or just agreed. This is the way men of all ages talk. How they talked yesterday, talk today and will probably talk tomorrow.

Occasionally, I walk into the trap myself. I constantly have to watch my tongue and pay attention to my behaviour. Comments like these are knee-jerk reactions.

The other day I told my wife about a managing director who had declined to join us to a bar after a board meeting. 'I bet he's not allowed to,' I added.

'What are you talking about? What do you know about that man and his family?' Greta asked.

She was right, of course. My comment must have been based on the assumption that he preferred to hang around with his colleagues instead of his wife and children. So, to choose to go home to one's family must be a sign of having a dominant wife – 'Not allowed to.' What did I actually mean? As I said, comments like this are knee-jerk reactions.

One day a thirty-two-year-old colleague called me and told me about a meeting he had just had.

'Did you know that their general manager is a woman? She looks like Dolly Parton. She's rather attractive, well, not as attractive as Dolly, and her breasts were smaller, of course. She wore a lot of make-up and is a little bit older, but nice.'

What are you supposed to reply to that? 'Did you make a deal?'

During board meetings, jokes about gays and women are very common. Nowadays, this makes me uncomfortable, and for the first time in fifty years I tell people off. 'Aren't we a little too old for these kind of jokes?'

'Yes, maybe you're right', someone might answer after a moment of silence. In that boardroom, we haven't made jokes about homosexuals or women since.

After that particular meeting, I was pleased with myself for having made my position clear, even though it shouldn't really be anything to brag about. It ought to go without saying that you must put your foot down when someone is crossing the line. This example shows that we men must accept our responsibility for making things happen regarding equality.

During a meeting with the board of an association working with women's questions, I was criticised by two members of the board for having taken an interest in equality matters. One of these women is a reader, the other a professor. They couldn't come to terms with the fact that a man, by himself, had taken an interest in and written about women and equality.

Isn't that peculiar? Questions regarding equality should be for women only to reflect on. But it shows that not just men are embedded in old habits and instinctively struggle to keep the status quo. I was really attacked during that meeting, but that was genuinely beneficial for the sexist in me.

Sleeping Her Way to the Top

I have heard many stories about women who have reached their positions through sex. I haven't got the faintest idea whether these are true or not. They are probably false. Have I forwarded such information? Yes, I have. Not as an intended strategy of mine, but as gossip, just for fun, between men. But perhaps it has been a kind of strategy, a sign of male weakness because these women have been more successful than me.

Many of the women I have interviewed while researching for this book have laughed about rumours that have been spread about them regarding affairs with their past bosses. There are always rumours going around about competent women, and the purpose of this is of course to hurt them and to prevent them from being promoted.

Ruler Techniques and a Collective Responsibility

Some time ago, I performed a number of consultant commissions for one of our major insurance companies. One day I was asked to look into a case of sexual harassment. It turned out that one of the managers had led a troop of younger men in bullying a female colleague. They chose to avoid her at lunchtime and sent porn pictures to her email address.

To me it seemed grotesque that adults should send porn pictures to a workmate and I hardly believed it. But it was true. After having investigated the matter, I suggested that the company should get rid of this oppressor. But my client told me that would be impossible because the matter was delicate. The man had strong bonds with the company, and he had been one of 'the company manager's boys'. Although this company manager had quit, it was an impossible step to take.

'You must understand, Lars, that we can't just get rid of such a guy.'

I honestly didn't understand why the company couldn't dismiss a person who harmed the organisation, the trademark, the colleagues and the atmosphere. But the matter came to nothing. We were not allowed to involve the union and everyone neglected their duties on all levels and in every possible way. I suffer from this case to this very day. I can't help thinking that I could have done more. This company never engaged me again; thank heavens for that.

'Hold the Mouse Nicely in Your Hand'

From my years in a world-leading computer company, I remember an embarrassing event that occurred in connection with a recruitment matter. A colleague received a woman applying for a managerial position. I attended this meeting, and the woman and I greeted each other in the reception.

I knew that my colleague wanted a man in this particular position. He asked the woman to sign in on the computer in the reception. He took the computer mouse (please note that in Swedish, the word for mouse also can mean pussy) in his hand, looked the woman straight in the eyes, smiled and said: 'Annika, that is your name, right? Look here. Grab the mouse and place it gently in your hand. Tickle it a little with your middle finger, nicely and gently. Feel it, take it easy, no sudden movements. Draw the finger upwards, then click.'

He continued like that for a while, still smiling. Neither I nor Annika knew what to do. Maybe I smiled too, but I hope by God I wasn't that gutless. However, Annika got the job and it turned out that she was exactly as competent as she had claimed. She was strong. Most applicants would have given up after that opening.

In one of the American offices of this computer company, several employees were engaged to work to combat sexual harassment. That function wasn't made available in any of the European offices, since we believed that we didn't have problems of that kind. But we had. In the European board of managers, there was a colleague who used to judge any woman by the amount of liquor he thought that he would have to drink to be willing to shag her.

Escort Service and Business Meetings

During my years in Paris and London, I realised how common it is to buy women, the so-called escort service. Wherever companies have their conferences, that line of business is flourishing.

I saw nothing strange in the fact that managers bought women. It was totally accepted. I remember a conference in southern France and how we laughed when some of the men wanted two women at a time. I laughed too, probably because I felt that I had no influence on the situation in either direction. It was too deeply rooted in the culture of the company and in the rules of the game.

Looking back, I realise that I could have expressed my feelings. I could have said that there is no way that I will accept this. I could have left the conference, which I have done on other occasions when the reason, compared to this, has been banal, such as poor conference management.

Swedish Companies

Is escort service a problem within Swedish companies too? That is hard to say. It's not that common in Sweden, but it occurs when men are out on business trips. It is rumoured that one of Sweden's biggest investment companies made it a habit during the eighties and nineties to invite their new male employees to a brothel or to offer escort service to them. This was a way to make young lads loyal. The national television company of Sweden has had its scandals. At one time a well-known talk-show host sexually harassed a female colleague. She was forced to quit and he was promoted.

It seems as if men are always innocent. They either remain in their positions or receive financial support as a compensation. Men can always claim that the whole thing is a mistake. Women are being pictured as unstable and emotional.

Men have a collective responsibility concerning sexism, harassment, prostitution and rape. All powerful groups have a responsibility. We have a collective responsibility for children, poverty, famine and the environment. The issue of equality is no exception.

In order to maintain human rights every action must be considered a good deed.

Ineffective Equality Plans

I can't remember one single company, nor one single management group, where equality has been made an issue. And yet I have been a member of around ten management groups and as a consultant have worked close to an additional twenty.

A minor exception was when a managing director of a media company, where I was assigned for six months, asked me to put together an equality plan, 'since the law requires that'. I called some old friends working in different companies as staff managers, and by email I received their different equality plans. By putting those together, I managed to produce a worthless document that we put away in a file somewhere.

The office of the equal opportunities ombudsman says that it is no crime if a company for some reason doesn't act according to the plan. They will get a reminder, that's all. So, the important thing is to have a plan, not to follow it.

Being reminded without punishment has no effect on men.

Equality Issues in My Professional Role

I have never been particularly active in bringing up issues about women's situations in the companies I have had a relationship with. I have never considered it necessary. I haven't looked upon it as a big issue or a problem. During hundreds of so-called working conferences I have discussed many companies' culture but never their view on equality. The issue has never been brought up, either by me, the company or the participants.

But a while ago on a conference I asked if the organisation that I worked with had a culture dominated by men. The women answered yes, loudly and with emphasis, whereas the men were puzzled and answered no, though hesitantly. Most of the men found it difficult to understand what it was within the company that could be macho. One of the men claimed that you can't change yourself, you are who you are.

Some years ago I worked, for the first time, with groups consisting of only women. An insurance company had asked me and two other consultants to work with self-confidence training. But although the course addressed women only, we never discussed the issue of equality. We mainly talked about issues in general such as why it is so difficult to say no, to claim your rights and to challenge all these things we feel obliged to do. We saw these problems as general problems, shared by men and women. No one brought up the male oppression and the male structure that rules. We, the consultants, did not and nor did our clients or the women. We were just touching the surface.

Some people claim that men have more self-confidence than women, and that is almost certainly due to the practice we men get throughout life, to command space and to be heard. Men are trained to get into conflicts, which means to win them, from your first football game at the age of five to who's taking the last bun at the coffee table in the old people's home. By contrast, women are trained to avoid conflicts, and if they do occur, to lose them. That strengthens the female identity. I know women who have been brought up to believe that the one who gives in is the best. To please men, a woman shall be cool, soft, cooperative, flexible, quiet, beautiful and blonde. That is part of the cliché men have about what a woman is and should be.

The Generation of Tomorrow

Women's Role at Home

Perhaps it is time to allocate men quotas in the kitchen. I mean on a daily basis, not just as barbecue chefs when friends are visiting in the summer. However, I doubt that men have the competence and the strength that is required to do two jobs.

Evidently, men are able to cook. Whenever a new restaurant is opening, you expect that the chef is a man. Men are the true masters of the kitchen. Men cook as a hobby, when friends are visiting or during weekends. And we are members of food and wine clubs.

Fish fingers on a Wednesday evening… no, thank you. The everyday kitchen life, we leave to women.

In the Fairy-Tale World

Many of the fairy tales we read to our children add to and confirm the picture of women as passive and bitchy. Little Red Riding Hood is a good example. She is so helpless and stupid that she can't see the difference between a disguised wolf and her grandmother – at least, not in the Swedish version of the book. However, in a recently printed Norwegian version the little girl eats the wolf and leaves the empty skin behind her in the snow as she walks away. Very symbolic, but differently so.

Snow White and Cinderella, with their longing and waiting, are just two of many examples of how early in life the slanted upbringing of girls starts. When we meet or read about strong and active women we picture them as dominant bitches. Even in real life we cultivate prejudices about the strong and dominant women. In the business world, 'iron lady' is a common epithet. And a successful Swedish businesswoman is sometimes referred to as Madam Saddam.

It is all about power. In our society, we reward powerful people (men), and we follow that norm with servility.

If I can't be the boss at work, maybe I can at home. Ranking orders are established wherever there is more than one person present. Two persons comprise a group and one of them will make the decisions.

The Perfect Naked Woman

I believe that young women of today experience more stress and pressure than ever before. And that is partly due to commercials, tabloids, youth culture, fashion magazines, music videos *et cetera*. It all points in the same direction. Women shall be pretty, fit, slim and, above all, nude. Media is full of rubbish, prejudices and a will to suppress the young generation to follow old conventions. 'Woman, stick to your last.'

How is it possible that some young, talented female athletes, artists or TV personalities are willing to undress if they get the opportunity to be on the cover of a magazine? I don't think it is about money. Rather it is about frustration and a search for an identity. 'Look at me now that I am naked. I'm a woman, am I not?'

And why is the suicide rate among young women escalating? Frustration? Confusion and lack of role models? Some female journalists are good role models and governments have made some attempts, but much more is required.

Obviously it is hard to be a young girl in society today. How do I know? Well, women have told me and I believe in what they have said. And I can think for myself. The enormous propaganda machine called publicity is welling up on us all the way into our hearts.

Much in society is unfair. I believe that the problems are accelerating, that girls and women of today are more pornographically exposed and violated now than for the past ten years. And I can't see any counter move.

It will be exciting, to say the least, to follow how women will be looked upon in the next generation. An undressed person is a vulnerable person, and keeping women undressed is to make them harmless. It is a method to see women as products that can be used whenever you want to. Men feel safer that way and can relax easier.

In Sweden it is not uncommon for female athletes to expose themselves in magazines. In March 2004 *Aftonbladet*, one of the leading newspapers in Sweden, asked the readers if it is all right for female football players in the national team to expose themselves in magazines. Seventeen-thousand people answered and 76% voted for the exposure.

Outdoor advertising companies allow pornographic magazines to advertise in the subway. Many men actually like pornographic magazines. It is pleasant to look at undressed models and it strengthens our profound opinion that all of them actually are whores. Except for my wife, of course, but the others are.

This will be interpreted as a pure provocation, I hope – not by men, they know how it is – but by many women. I know several men who feel uncomfortable about seeing lightly dressed men in advertisements. We tend to believe that male models are all gay. Our problem is where to place talented football players like Fredrik Ljungberg and David Beckham, who are successful models for famous fashion trademarks.

The New Generations

At a seminar in 2004, the differences between people born in the forties and in the seventies came up. The issue was whether there will be more equality with a younger generation in charge. Unfortunately, the framing of the question was totally wrong. There will be no such transition as new people are filling up all the time.

I can't remember when I last got an application from someone born in the forties. The people in charge today were born in the sixties, and those born in the seventies are already on their way to take over. The headhunters, the recruiters, will soon be looking out for the new generation, born in the eighties – hungry, strong guys (and girls) who can sell, work their hearts out and take new shares of the market.

Many, all too many, of the young men I meet in the business

world today think the way I did when it comes to male/female matters. They have same attitudes, the same prejudices. It makes you wonder why so many young men don't ponder their behaviour, although they are raised in a society that is more equally oriented. I believe that it often comes down to a lingo, an attitude, which will facilitate entry into the male fellowship. The younger men wish to show solidarity and loyalty to us silverbacks by laughing along to woman-degrading jokes and sustaining the atmosphere. They make jokes about women, gays and immigrants but don't actually mean what they are saying.

The barrack room lingo works efficiently as ruler technique. The problem with jokes is that they stick and develop into truths. The adjustment into the male society has always worked this way. All youngsters, class of society irrelevant, have been taught this way.

Turned Tables

For a few years I lived and worked both in London and in Stockholm. No one paid much attention to that in spite of the fact that my wife Greta for periods of time lived by herself in Stockholm. Most of my friends thought that the London thing was cool, and it gave a little extra weight to my consultant status. Many thought that it was nice for Greta as well. Imagine having apartments both in Stockholm and London! What a dream, and what opportunities for shopping!

Some time after my moving back to Sweden, Greta took a job in the town of Karlstad close to the Norwegian border. Consequently, she commuted to and from Stockholm. The same friends who had thought that my commuting to London was cool now reacted quite differently. The women looked at me with wet eyes and wondered if I could cope with the situation. Our male friends reacted differently. They raised their eyebrows and looked knowingly at me: 'Alone all week! My, my...'

One friend suggested an excellent laundry for a poor grass widower. And wouldn't it be more practical if I had my meals at the little restaurant nearby? Lilian, a lady of a certain age, works there and she has practically adopted me already. Whenever I order a shrimp sandwich or something she asks me if I have been a good boy. I always assure her that I have and then I feel good about myself for the rest of the day. I am a good boy of about fifty with too heavy demands on myself, transplanted by a male society that I no longer understand and no longer know if I want to be part of.

So, I was left responsible for our home when Greta left for Karlstad. It was really no big deal. It was me and my at-the-time seventeen-year-old daughter who lived in the flat during the weekdays. I cleaned on Fridays, bought something nice for dinner and rented a film for the evening.

At the beginning, Greta appreciated this, and while we sat down at the dinner table she told us all about her exciting week, her journeys and about people she had met. Sometimes she had bought me a gift. She thought I had done well with the household.

I felt good about that, but after some time this appreciation stopped. She talked more and more about her own problems and challenges. She didn't notice the efforts I had made in the apartment. I was working too, of course, but I didn't have to travel so I was at home in the evenings.

It took a while before I realised that my work was overshadowed by hers. This was a new experience for me and eventually I had to point out that I had cleaned our flat. Greta congratulated me and told me I had been a good boy, but it disturbed me that I had to remind her.

Over time, I realised that she acted like a man. I recognised myself from my earlier marriage. In those days, I was the one who was travelling and my wife, the mother of our two children, was the one who took care of the household and raised the children. More and more I realised what her life had been like and how I had acted. Like a real chauvinist pig.

This was a good, as well as a sad, insight, and it strongly contributed to my rethinking about manhood and womanhood. I remembered shamefully that one of my demands when we were planning to have children was that she became a housewife. I had to take care of my career and couldn't be disturbed by infants.

Now I realise that my oppressing attitude for many years

stopped her from doing what she wanted to do. And at that time, I saw nothing wrong in this. I felt pride in not having taken time off to be with my children when they were small. I was proud to make a career, proud to earn good money. If possible, my mother was even more proud.

I realise now that I never took part in the upbringing of my children. I was just some kind of subsidiary character. My daughter Jenny used to say that she only recalls me being at home at the weekends. I know she is right. I wasn't present. And if I was at home, I was engaged in my work.

Generally, my son Jacob agrees to that, but being a young man he has a more understanding attitude to this. He wants to become a manager himself one day, to reach higher levels than I have and to make more money.

In one way I don't regret my behaviour. I wouldn't have had the patience to spend more time with my children. It would have demanded too much of me. Too much work and too little self-realisation. It wouldn't have suited me. But, as I said, my opinion was that it suited my wife.

I can only hope that if and when my children become parents, they will find other ways of life and value things other than that which I have done.

In an Equal Society, We Are All Winners

The fact that Sweden has reached certain levels of equality is nothing to be high and mighty about. The present officer of the equal opportunities ombudsman in Sweden, Claes Borgstrom, has said that 'Either it's equal or it isn't.' There is no compromise.

In spite of this, I would like to say something about the leisurely progress of equality. There is resistance everywhere, from both men and women. People have an inherent resistance to changes, so from that perspective one shouldn't feel low-spirited.

When I meet businessmen today and ask if they can consider a woman on the position that is to be filled, I am serious, and so are many managers. The idea that no women are willing to be managers or that they are difficult to find is just lies. It all depends on where you are looking.

The slowness of this process is due to the fact that changes in attitude and behaviour are extremely difficult to work with. What a person says is not always what he means.

But before we accuse men of being conservative, we have to consider that men, and women too, are formed from hundreds of years of oppression and prejudices of standards and misconceptions. It's a kind of brainwash, even if we don't want to use that word. The Church, as well as the bourgeois dream of the happy nuclear family, is an example of institutions and phenomena that have prevented equality.

To keep the changing process going from one generation to the other, we have to initiate conversations about equality in our homes, in nursery school, in comprehensive school and in our places of work.

The Evolution of Women

The women of today in Sweden will start a revolution, simply because we have a system where men rule and women obey. The evolution will not arise as in the old days with sex strikes and other militant actions; it will be more through a process where women will get access to the structures of power and piece-by-piece change our everyday life. It will take time, but it will be worth it.

A small majority of Sweden's inhabitants are women, but only a few are heard in the debates. But the number will increase and the penetrative power will grow. The issue of equality will not fade and will not go out of fashion.

What is needed is a more collective movement and I am sure it will come. A scattered movement making selective contributions will never have any lasting influence on society in general. A united movement, on the other hand, could work miracles.

To future generations of women, female role models together with legislation will be determining. But I maintain that the initiative must come from women themselves.

Advantages at Home

In an equal society, man can be pictured as the loser. He loses many privileges, he gets a lot of extra work (domestic) and when applying for a managerial position he will find that the competition has increased. But according to some, men will also gain a lot. To be honest, I don't know what.

One thing I do know for sure, though: it brings a lot of joy not to be an oppressor. It makes life easier to live. When you lie down in bed at night, it feels so much better to know that you have done your best to communicate and cooperate during the day.

In a more equal society, men will definitely get less time to ourselves. But we will spend more time with our children, our homes and our families. Unfortunately, there will also be some boring tasks like laundry, shopping and cleaning. Trivialities? Not at all, contrary to what most men think. I am sure that most women who are responsible for the homes (almost 100%, I believe) find it important to discuss who is going to take care of what in the household.

Oh my God, my fellow brothers might sigh, equality can't be all about such trivial things. For heaven's sake, the washing-up and the shopping can't be anything to argue about…

Men might help once in a while with these tasks but to carry the responsibility all together, never. We would rather eat out, taking care of the laundry only when absolutely necessary, or getting help elsewhere.

Advantages in Business Life

I find it easier to survey the benefit of equality within trade and industry. I believe that there would be an improvement in many areas if we were more equal and treated each other with more respect and in a more relaxed way.

In mixed groups, the atmosphere is more exciting and dynamic. If you are in a minority at meetings, your items seem to fall off the agenda and never turn up again. Unless, that is, you are a very powerful woman or get along well with the boss.

In the field of recruiting, we preach about the power of differences. But what we really talk about is peoples of the same sex, i.e. men, who are not acting like the boss. However, it is welcomed if the candidates share background, values and interests with him.

The differences between male and female thinking are, as most of us understand, considerable. Men and women have different experiences and together we might find a third road that leads to more understanding.

Leadership changes radically in heterogeneous groups. The language becomes more serious, clear and varied. And being a group leader, you are forced to look at issues from different angles. On the whole, results improve and solutions to problems are more genuine and long-ranged. This has a significant impact on successful projects.

A bunch of men might thump each other on the back about a taken decision and say 'Let's go for it' without reflecting over weaknesses or difficulties. In a homogeneous group, you tend to be blindfolded. With more women in the group it is easier to take up problems from the start and things are planned in a more realistic way.

In heterogeneous groups the credibility of taken decisions increases and it is easier to stick to them. And the trademark, the image of the company, is fortified and clarified. If you address people of both sexes with your products, it would be strange if you don't have people of both sexes, on all levels, producing them.

Three Problems That Must Be Solved

The first problem that needs to be solved is the difference in wages. You are valued as a person by your salary, not by your bonuses or your options (very few of us have any bonuses). The monthly pay cheque is what counts. That's what shows how much you are worth as a human being and how you are valued by your employer. Consequently, people who work with children are less valued than those who work with money, drugs and weapons. Why? Children have never had a high status. In general, men are not interested in working with children, including their own. What men say about quality time as opposed to quantity time is sheer nonsense. Men don't prefer to spend time with their child, that's the plain truth. And it has most likely to do with genes as well as environmental influence.

The second problem concerns what men would gain in a more equal society. This is an important issue, both from economical and social aspects. To men, increased equality, in the sense that we respect each other regardless of sex and that we cooperate, would lead to a broadened outlook on social relations as well as to development of business life. The effect on social relations is easy to understand. But development of business life? What a challenging thought.

In the middle of the eighties, I thought we were on our way. Books about femininity and masculinity were written and the subject was often an issue in seminars. Most managers were men, of course, and it became fashionable to talk about the androgynous manager, a man who uses his feminine side in order to gain what is called better social competence. Nothing really came of the creation of the androgynous manager, as far as I know. I suppose the only people who gained anything from the whole thing were us consultants. At least we made some money.

The next time I sensed a change was at the beginning of the nineties when we started to talk about 'The Good Citizen Company'. Companies and organisations were supposed to accept their responsibility and support weaker groups: for example, to give away part of the profit to the Third World or to make it possible for female staff members to carry out certain activities. Apple, for instance, donated old computers to Eastern Europe and the Swedish State Railways encouraged female employees to participate in a big bicycle race in Stockholm, raising money for environmental causes.

In those days, I thought women would take a step forward, but that didn't happen. And yet the concept of the good, responsible company seemed fit for women to take place in, since it was based on welfare and sponsorship.

In all the management groups and development projects with which I have been involved, the discussions have been widened and broadened when women have been present. That is a fact. On the other hand, it has taken more time, initially, to reach decisions. But the projects have undoubtedly been more thought-out and better understood.

The third problem is, of course, what women can gain from increased equality. And what do they risk? The benefit is obvious. They will experience advantages that we men have always experienced. Fewer diapers, more golf. Time for a glass of wine with friends in a cosy restaurant, watching handsome guys by the bar. Or whatever they decide to do.

One thing is obvious. If we are going to share more of the responsibility for the contents of our lives, women will start to take their share of the apple and we men will initially feel like losers. Why? Because we will be losers. Hundreds of years of oppression and bullying will come to an end and we will have to learn other ways of behaviour and to respect people.

Society as a whole will gain from this and we men will have to fight on new grounds and lose jobs to women because they are more competent. A cruel fate.

I think that women of tomorrow will suffer from seeing much less of their children. Of course, career women of today already have made that sacrifice, just as we men have done. I myself never felt guilty about this since our children were in safe hands with their mother.

All women won't be winners. Some are always losers. Some-one has to take care of the children and someone has to take care of the household, but in Sweden the new government thinks that the new way will be to hire someone to take care of the running of the household for you.

Oppression and Feminism

Assumption of Power

> Are women free to make a career? To reach the top? Hardly.
> Some are, apparently, but then it is asserted that she has chosen
> career before children.

This was written in a business magazine when one of the major
banks in Sweden appointed a female top director. So, what are
they going to write now when she both has children and has
become manager of the whole concern?

Fundamentally, all women are feminists. At least, they should
be. Or is that too far-fetched? I don't think so. Show me the
woman that would state that Lena Gemzoe – researcher at Centrum
för Kvinnoforskning, an institute for womanhood research at the
University of Stockholm – is wrong in her definition. She claims
that a feminist is a person who believes that:

1. Women are subordinate to men.
2. That must be changed.

But still, you sometimes meet women who say they are not
feminists. How is that possible? Well, it is probably the same old
story. The women want to protect the men.

Feminism and feminist are two detestable words to many
men. It threatens their own position of power. That is one of the
conclusion I have drawn after making interviews and examining
research. But to protect your position is not a solely male
behaviour, rather a human one.

I have earlier mentioned that I consider women to be strong
and men to be dominant. Why, then, are women strong? Mainly

because women can talk about emotions and show emotions. And they strive to solve conflicts in a way that makes anyone who is engaged in the debate consider himself a winner. That is certainly a quality that not all men have. Most men want to win, dominate and steamroll. Emotions and conflicts are uncomfortable elements and should be handled by other people. Like women.

At the companies where I have been involved in one way or another, women have had to find solutions to the really tough questions – the questions considered to be 'soft', such as conflicts, cultural differences and changing processes.

In 2003, Jennie Sjogren wrote the book *Ordination: Vardagsfeminism* (*Everyday Feminism*) which ought to be compulsory reading in comprehensive school for both girls and boys. From this book I have borrowed certain definitions of subordination that I find very interesting. All the comments within brackets are my own.

There are four spheres in society where the subordination of women in comparison to men is obvious:

1. Politics and economy

Women are under-represented in many areas. The labour market is highly segregated gender-wise, especially within the sectors of finance and economy and health and care.

2. Family

Housework and childcare are mainly performed by women. Men use about 12% of their parental leave. [Usually around Christmas, New Year and during the summer when women usually are free anyway, which means they can share the work. It is not unusual that his mother gives a helping hand during these periods!]

3. Culture

In this area, work by women is generally being degraded. Trades like media, advertising and fashion are built on the condition that women are objectified. The passive, soft-porn pictures meet us everywhere. [It is actually getting a bit tiresome and many men claim that they have had enough of this.]

4.   Violence

Sexual crimes and assault against women and children are the most obvious and brutal forms of oppression towards women. Considering the effects, society takes surprisingly few measures to solve crimes like these. [For the first time in Sweden, a man was recently convicted for assaulting children because they had witnessed him beating their mother. A breakthrough!]

I agree with all this myself, but I am no feminist. Unfortunately. Not a genuine one, anyway. I am rather a macho copy trying to stick to human values, such as that we all ought to be equal and have the same privileges. But it is so easy to fail your standards. I myself walk into the pitfall every day, climb up and try again. To change attitudes and behaviour is extremely difficult and can't be achieved overnight, perhaps not even during a generation.

Many male politicians claim to be feminists, but that is usually only a way to get more votes, or an attempt to be a modern leader. Fundamentally, it means nothing. Jan Guillou, a Swedish journalist and author, has written that he called himself a feminist until he heard that Goran Persson, the former prime minister of Sweden, also did. According to Guillou, the word then lost all its significance. I tend to agree.

The question is rather whether any of these two macho icons can call himself feminist at all. If we once again look at Gemzoe's definition, she claims that a feminist considers women to be subordinated to men and that this should be changed.

Guillou carries and Persson used to carry enough power to enable these changes. Goran Persson was a prime minister with a considerable amount of power, symbolically as well as legally. Jan Guillou is one of the most influential journalists and debaters in Sweden. Is it possible to carry so much power and still be a feminist? To be in favour of changes in the power structure between the sexes? That's an interesting question.

Jan Guillou and Goran Persson are two of the most admired people in Sweden. They are always on top of the lists when institutes, papers and magazines invite voting or valuations of that kind. What symbolic value is there to feminism when men like this call themselves feminists? Is it a positive thing or does it undermine the concept? What active measures have they taken from their positions? And what significance has it had?

Some people claim that the woman is the stronger in a relationship (but the man is the dominant, I maintain).

Harriet Goldhor Lerner refers to Alice Miller and claims that women always protect men, no matter what. And that men are seeking a new mother when they are looking for a woman to marry. The Swedish author and feminist Nina Björk describes the same processes in her book *Under det rosa täcket*, (*Under the Pink Cover*). Women who walk out of a relationship are considerably few, an insignificant percentage. Women put up with things hoping it will get better. It won't. Nothing gets better by itself. Ask all the assaulted women. Or ask the politician Maria Carlshamre, a really strong, independent woman who one day decided to walk away from her oppressor and make a career for herself. She got a surprisingly high number of votes in the European Parliament election in 2004 and I think that is because both men and women considered her strong and impressive because she had managed to turn her back on her tormentor.

She is a clever person too, but I think that was secondary in this case. She rose and we tend to admire that kind of strength.

Female Oppression and Violence

The law against heinous female violation came in 1998 as an aid to women who were subject to repeated assault, a crime that can carry up to six years of imprisonment. That is almost never given as a sentence. Only one third of the assault cases lead to prosecution. In Sweden, the police have been assigned more than five million dollars extra in order to learn more about this kind of criminality.

According to prosecutors, it is very important that the interrogations of the victims are recorded on video in order to strengthen the women when the trial later takes place. But this happens very rarely. Why?

In a TV interview, a police officer said that 'We often forget to start the camera.' A prosecutor admitted in the same TV programme that it is common to shut down assault cases if the victim is too eager to have the man prosecuted. To obtain redress and a trial, the women are told to be 'moderate, because then you will be believed'.

Women who are too demonstrative or independent are considered to desire vengeance and the courts don't approve of that. Another problem is that some women withdraw their reports, i.e. are too passive. The courts don't approve of that either.

In other words, you are supposed to be moderately cooperative. A little submissive but still firm, strong but a little weak, quiet but plain speaking. In short, to act the way you are expected as a woman.

From Jennie Sjogren's book *Ordination: Vardagsfeminism* (*Everyday Feminism*) I pick a few facts:

> Women in the European Union perform 80% of household work, even when they work outside of home (Women's Lobby 2001).

> Of women between eighteen and thirty-four years, 64% have been sexually harassed some time.

The same night, I watched a TV programme where some 'famous' Swedes talked about different gender issues. One of the people around the table, a well-known politician, said, 'I stay out of this contraceptive tablet discussion, that's a female matter.' Not one of the four women around the table, of which one was the Swedish family minister, reacted.

Female Enterprise

It takes specific female qualities, like intuition and creativity, to refine a business idea. And yet it happens that a woman who wants to start a company is asked if her husband knows about the whole thing. This question is asked at the bank, but also in private life. What is your husband's opinion about this? Not many men are asked what their wives think when one of them announces that he is thinking about going into business.

But maybe a new attitude is emerging. Female entrepreneurs are building a reputation of their own, a good reputation. It's obvious who are lying, bluffing and stealing. It is, as you realise, the men.

Women rarely let their companies go bankrupt. Unlike men, they put their business in order before shutting the company down.

Prejudice against Men and Women

In October 2003, I went to see a female psychic in Stockholm. She gave me a lesson in psychology. She was around forty years old and told me that men, people like me, are active and go getting. 'Fight and flight' are male qualities and have so been since 'a bear was sitting in front of my cave'. Women are passive and protective, 'rest and digest'. The health prophet also found it amusing that the phrases rhyme: 'easier to remember'. And I couldn't disagree with that.

I suggested that I could fool the bear by throwing a piece of meat to the left of the opening and running at full speed to the right. If I wished to get out, that is. 'There you are,' said the health prophet, 'you are already busy trying to find a solution.'

Protect the myths, I thought.

I staggered out and walked shaken (well, a bit) down the street, thinking, 'are those prejudices still present?' Because they are prejudices, aren't they?

Well, that depends on whom you are asking. I know psychologists who would agree to that we have remained on the Stone Age level.

In April 2004, a major tabloid in Stockholm published an article in which you could read that men are unable to iron their shirts because they are hunters and are constantly on the move. Nor do the men, according to the article, observe when their home is untidy and dirty since their sense of smell is inferior to women's. The statement originates from the American family therapist Michael Gurian.

What are you supposed to think? I mean, where are those so-called truths leading us? What fruit do they bear? I can't see anything but a confirmation of our roles and that nothing will develop. The differences between men and women are obvious, aren't they? And, honestly, why leave the cave if there is a bear out there? Oh my, I don't know. I would remain in there until he gave up the waiting.

The same goes for the dirty linen. I prefer sitting by the TV with a beer and some snacks to standing in the basement, sorting dirty clothes. Anything peculiar about that? I don't think so. Women share the same preferences but have almost never any choice.

Sitting on the train between Karlstad and Stockholm one September day, I watch a mother with two children on the opposite seat. During the three-hour-long journey she is fully occupied, to say the least. She works intensively to feed, comfort and entertain. Once in a while her cellphone rings. It is probably her husband saying a few supporting words. The energy and the toil that this woman puts me to shame. I wouldn't have stood it, that's for sure.

Are Women Dangerous?

Yes, of course they are. Not as assailants; in those statistics they are almost absent. But definitely as competitors in working life. In recruitment as well as in the framing of questions in a management group, they would constitute a major threat if we were recruiting widely and asked for competence instead of gender. It would mean twice as many candidates to every position.

For a period of time, some women were considered so dangerous that they were burnt at the stake. They were called witches, and that epithet justified all forms of torture, oppression, hunting and extermination. Nowadays, we burn the women with new methods, from sophisticated, stealthy tricks at work to gang rapes.

Male ruler techniques:

1. To make you invisible. You simply aren't there or are forgotten.

2. To ridicule. Your comments are joked about.

3. To withdraw information. You are served with blurry information or are kept out all together.

4. To punish you in two ways. Whatever you do, it turns out wrong.

5. To make you feel guilty or shameful. A combination of ridicule and double punishment.

This list is a sad one, and still all five techniques are clearly recognisable. I have used them myself, but most of all I have seen them being practised in business life.

Saddest of all is maybe that a young woman like Jennie Sjogren in the year 2003 has to sit down and write a book about ruler techniques. So we have reached no further than that. After having met Ida Larsson and Amanda Svensson, two women engaged in the same area, I have learnt that the list of ruler techniques has now been increased to nine. That is an interesting fact in itself, but I doubt that it will make us any happier. It reminds me of old Freud's theory of defence mechanisms. They were around ten in the beginning, but fifty years after his death the number was several hundred.

When we in the western world brag about how much more equal society has become, we must remember that we talk about a minority of the population of the world – not even 1%. In most parts of the world, the oppression of women can only be suspected or read about. Punishments like stoning and gang rape can be given as a sentence if a woman is as much as suspected of committing adultery.

That kind of culture affects us all, regardless of where we live. There is a message that goes straight into your consciousness. Or are there people who believe that we aren't affected? In that case, why would commercials and propaganda influence people over borders?

Men's Fear

Gang rapes have become more and more common in Sweden, and the perpetrators get ever younger. This is alarmingly serious; especially if you consider that it seldom leads to any convictions.

Whatever the reason for the increase, it is a very odd phenomenon, and it must come to an end now. The signal you send out to young boys is totally wrong when nothing happens, and somehow all men receive some kind of message that rape is no big deal. When the penalty for drink driving can be more severe than for gang rape (maybe not theoretically, but in reality), it sends out certain signals to young man and to society in general.

Many men feel uncomfortable in the presence of women. They imagine women to be dangerous. One way for confused young men to 'socialise' with women can be to do it gang wise. A gang rape is both an assault and abuse of power.

At divorces, men are humorously said to be interested in two items that mean a lot to them: the boat and the car. The man usually looks upon himself as the one who has paid for stuff like that and 'forgets' that his wife's money has been spent on food and clothes for the children.

If children are involved, the court usually decides that the woman shall keep the house or the apartment. The children are left to her with a minimum of discussion and this is rarely looked upon as a sacrifice by the man. Children amount to extra work, a burden to the man in his future life and career. Men fight for their right of parental access, and are of course entitled to that if they have conducted themselves properly before, but men don't want the main responsibility for the children. Not a chance!

I've never heard of a man who is prepared to fight for anything better than the right to spend time with the children every other week. If the man is awarded or fights for total access, it usually means that something is seriously wrong with the woman – it might indicate alcohol or drug abuse, or if she has 'abandoned' home. Which, by the way, is what so many men have done through history.

Men are the losers in the long run. Solitary men are usually unable to win the last round. Almost every week, reports occur of violence against women and other kinds of oppression in working places and homes. And for ten or fifteen years, genital invectives have been accepted in school, towards pupils as well as teachers. Accepted? Yes, otherwise they wouldn't occur. Using that kind of language would be punished, and punished hard.

What is the penalty rate like? There is none. There is hardly a penalty even for rape. Does this affect our view of women? Of course it does. We are all affected, young as well as old. The signals are as effective as in an advertising campaign.

It is odd that we believe that only advertisements affect our view on women. The general idea is to oppress women, and in that ambition, all the different parts of society cooperate with 'the market' in a most brilliant way.

The truth is that everything we do, all actions in everyday life, at work and in the intercourse with our children, sets those mind patterns that boys as well as girls grow accustomed to for the rest of their lives. And than we stand there with the new pamphlets from the department of health and education, scratching the back of our heads, saying, 'Why, everybody's got the pamphlet and the problem has been addressed in school, so why don't they do as they've been told?'

No, I don't believe that women are dangerous in themselves; on the contrary. But they do indeed threaten our positions. And, as in history between all nationalities and groups, there will be war when the ruling section of society is being challenged. We are in the middle of that war, and the question is who will win. Men, women or all of us?

Women sometimes claim that we should fight together and that men and women can build something new, on new conditions. We men will assist when we realise that we have no choice and that we can benefit from a change. But very few really like change. Just think about how difficult it is to abolish a coffee break at work, to decrease an allowance or to demand that a person will arrive in time.

Madeleine Leijonhufvud is a Swedish professor of penal law. She states that:

> In the recent years, there has occurred an adjustment in favour of the belief among courts that women enjoy sex with several men at the same time. The circumstances can sometimes be so absurd that you can hardly avoid being sarcastic.

Most rapes are committed at home or at least by a perpetrator known by the woman. This fact is ever-present as a threat to all women and as a weapon in the heads of all men. Naturally, most men don't go the whole hog, but the threat is always there. Consequently, the old threat to burn the witch also remains, and the danger is exceedingly real. A raped woman becomes stigmatised and as burned as if she had been tied to the stake. You may think that we have gone beyond that in the twenty first century, but we haven't.

Structures

There is an obvious trend in Sweden today for politicians to present themselves as feminists. All of them want that, and maybe not just as a method to attract voters.

Gudrun Schyman is the former leader of the socialist Left Party in Sweden. She is the one who has been most eager and who has been hit back at most of all. When she compared the Taliban to Swedish men, claiming that the oppression patterns are practically identical, she was harshly attacked. The male society took a real blow and retaliated. But she was right. The structures are the same, because there is just one kind of oppression structure.

Structures are, however, multiple in the brains of us men. For one thing, we sincerely believe that when you speak the word 'person', you mean 'man'. Man is strong, man makes the decisions. In other words, there are people: men; and then there are the others: women. This, too, is a 'Taliban' structure, rooted in our backbone. It is a difficult task to remove it.

Many a time this becomes obvious when men talk in private. The objectification of women among us men today is as strong as ever. Nothing has changed. Good enough, not good enough – the constant foundations of judgement are not based on intellect, only on looks and manners. Friendly and courteous are female characteristics, questioning and dominant are male. And, if a woman acts that way, she is difficult to handle.

In 1998, the High Commissioner for Human Rights of the United Nations, Mary Robinson, made the announcement that 'human rights are also female rights'. And she wasn't referring to the so-called Third World, the developing countries; she was talking about us all. In 1998!

Man's strength is purely muscular, and both sexes are aware of that. A latent threat is ever-present in all relations and situations – always, at least in the male mind. The ancient male threat to leave his woman and move out is just as common today as it was a hundred years ago. And it still works; the women stay quiet. No one wants to be left alone, and the men use this usually empty threat merely to increase their power.

But women are rarely left alone in the long run. All research shows that women tend to find themselves a new life after a divorce, a life with many dimensions and friendships, while men try to find a new woman as soon as possible. Actually, the women have probably kept their social networks through the relationship, while men have lost theirs.

So, women, rise and leave your men unless you are treated as equals. Don't hang on to the 'wrong' man; that won't strengthen you and you will end up in a blind alley.

The Leader/Manager Role and Success

Visions and Success

There are may talented Swedes, both males and females. The most exciting personalities are perhaps those who have started with empty hands and managed to carry out their visions. So what are visions?

In fact, there are indications that visions have a biological base. According to David Ingvar, a former professor of clinical neurophysiology, you can observe a development of heat in the brain when some people think of the future. A visionary person's brain actually changes due to an increase of heat in the frontal lobes. Ingvar describes visions as memories of the future. Isn't that beautiful? Memories of the future. Those who have visions and the strength to guide themselves and the rest of us forward have already been there and taken a glance.

The heptathlete Carolina Kluft, the alpine skier Anja Parson and the rider Malin Bayard are three of the greatest Swedish athletes ever. They all are world-class performers within their discipline. They all have a passion and motivation that has taken them through lonely training hours, day after day, week after week, month after month. They all seem outgoing, happy and obliging.

What has driven them? The same motivation as for men? That's difficult to know. But they seem to have one thing in common: they thank their fathers.

Have you ever heard a male athlete refer his success to a woman? No, never. The media often claims the opposite. When Björn Borg and Ingemar Stenmark had down periods in their careers, you could read that their concentration was disturbed by women. We are not born with equal possibilities. The idea about the equal society is only a tall tale, maintained by those who have all the opportunities in life, not by the others. Many of those on the losing side realise that it's no use. Just trying to make a career would seem like a stupid idea – not least for women.

But those in power within politics and business always think it is picturesque if some underdog plays a part in the debate. And the media love them. However, in Sweden, the humble suburbs won't be where new female managers will develop their talents. The ruling class and its offspring live in other areas and enjoy privileges that most people only can dream about.

But if a new movement arises in the concrete suburbs and a strong woman (or maybe a few) steps forward, we will experience a kind of revolution that could be sensational. Because out in the suburbs you can find strength, energy, revenge, hunger and aggression. All societies are strictly patterned in different levels and classes. Networks, gender and environment are important parameters. An untalented man might, if his father has the right position, be assigned the top spot, and there is nothing we can do about it if the old man is powerful enough.

Of course, this goes for women, too. Networks, structures, opportunities and conditions are to some extent evident. Sometimes the system allows an underdog to break through, because it is quaintly pleasing or because the exception proves the rule.

The Leader

It is a common mistake to connect leadership to management. There is no such obvious connection. You are appointed to the right to be a manager, but you seize the right to be a leader.

1. Leaders are followed, and they leave those who can't cope behind. Leadership is about to advance from thought to action, which is something most of us never do. Just the visionaries have the guts and the stamina.

2. Managers give orders with indirect or direct threats of sanctions. To have the power to control somebody else's salary is an effective instrument, to be able to sack a person is another. Without these instruments, most managers would fail. The threat of sanctions is what pushes most of us and keeps the society structure in check.

A common problem for leaders seems to be that they know too little about what happens in the nearest surroundings. The reason is probably that successful people don't listen too carefully to their advisers. They have a sceptical attitude towards people around them and seem to think, why listen to someone who isn't as successful as I am? Since I am the best and he's not, why should I take any advice from him?

There are many examples of visionaries, leaders and artists who make their own rules. And there are also athletes who create their own training methods, not caring about what the manual says. They are usually the most successful. They stretch the boundaries, create new patterns and refuse to see the limits. In our fear of divergent behaviour, we try to persuade young people to go their own ways, just as long as they do what we tell them. Thereby, we also throttle many talented people's creativity. Those who have the strength to resist and find their own ways are those who eventually will be standing at the top.

A newly appointed manager enters an existing environment, studies the organisation schedules and creates his platform in the hierarchy. A newly appointed leader starts by remaking the entire organisation so it suits him and his ambitions. Or hers, of course. This is regardless of which position he has within the structure. Even if our leader hasn't a managerial position, he or she makes sure that the structure is changed in a way that makes them happy and gets as much as possible out of the others. All in order to realise his own very private goals.

The entrepreneur just doesn't see any limits. If you can't go around, over or under the obstacle, well, you'll just have to go over it.

'But that's not possible,' I object.

'Well, I have to do something,' the entrepreneur would say.

Most others would give up. But to entrepreneurs, resignation is not an option. That's the foundation of enterprise.

People are different. And unusually successful people are often extreme in social life. They challenge ordinary people's actions and thinking. Entrepreneurs are exactly what we need in the equality process in order to achieve success.

Groups look for and can choose leaders, but that isn't done at random. The potential leaders see to it that they are selected, which is a step in a deliberate process that they use to reach higher positions.

Women are, from a general point of view, not used to that kind of system. Men have practised since early age and know that someone makes the decisions and that someone will be excluded. Men always compete. It could start with arm wrestling at home with dad in the kitchen, and then its football, ice hockey, baseball, noughts and crosses or wrestling in the schoolyard. Women don't compete, they cooperate, starting with assisting mum in the kitchen.

Leaders choose their flock, and they do it by using power, strength, aggression and lies – if necessary. A flock doesn't choose leaders, that sustains an old prejudice. It's difficult to make a top career if you can't be ruthless and are able to put emotions aside. Considerate emotionalists become welfare officers, not great leaders or managers.

Male leaders who are emotionally oriented are often described as coaches, team leaders, judges of character and other positive terms. Female leaders with the same qualities are described as unfocused, incapable of making quick decisions, dependent and so on.

The Achievement and Sacrifices of the Leader

Power is something you can achieve by accomplishment, unless you inherit it. But inherited power is often accompanied by contempt. What you haven't deserved, you shouldn't possess. It's part of our civilisation to observe injustices, even though we put the lid on our thoughts in larger companies.

At heart, we all have resources to achieve top results, but just a few make it. Those people show the ability to focus their energy, guide themselves and develop. This is most obvious within culture and sports, but naturally it exists in business life and official administration as well.

It goes without saying that the only way to attain development and achievement, permanent change and a good life is to interact and grow in the company of others. You can't achieve anything if you don't stimulate and help each other.

Women may have a tendency to choose an easy way out, but that could be because they are fed up with us men. Or perhaps they believe that courses in personality development will help them in their already difficult task to make us go along with them. I know women who attend courses and then send their husbands to them.

If you really want to achieve more than others, you must be prepared to put everything else aside – your family as well as your hobbies. Rumour has it that some big-shot businessmen see their children only in limousines between their homes and airports and in some cases there may be an element of truth in it. However else could they find the time for it? I happen to know that Mick Jagger spends hours a day on the phone, talking to his children. Obviously, it's the only chance. Most climbers prefer loneliness before ordinary family life in order to reach fame and glory.

A successful female manager said in a TV interview that she had a helpful husband, domestic help and a nanny. She also said that she wished that 'all women should have such assistance… well, maybe not everyone.' And she put her finger on a problem there! Everyone can't employ a domestic help, for who helps the domestic help in that case?

Leader Types

The Male Leader – The Dictator

The most worrying factor about leadership is that the most successful companies are most often ruled by dictators – at least in times past. These dictators are men who interfere with every little detail and are ruthless in their drive to be successful. The motivation isn't money but power and control, satisfaction in success, the wonderful feeling of forcing yourself and others to the utmost. The most successful leadership style is by no means the one we read about in all the management books discussing coaching and social competence. Why do I claim this? Well, think of all the successful companies that have earned a place at the top, small as well as big. The leader, the visionary, uses a group as long as he needs it. He quickly exchanges members of the group if he regards someone as inadequate. Women are less likely to accept that kind of ruthless mechanisms. Female leaders usually try to find solutions that don't involve hurting anybody. See to the group as a whole first: build up, find a solution; behave unmanfully, in other words, and don't be very career-oriented.

Men play off against each other and try to find holds on rivals. Since you never know when someone will go behind your back, you might as well be prepared all the time. That, my friends, is to make a career.

What do these men have in common? Well, they have a militant attitude, are ruthless in relations but social when they want to and when it is useful. They demand everything from their employees, and if you don't play along, you're fired. Conditional love, ultimatum. Unpleasant but very successful.

I have met quite a few of these men and worked with some of them. Most of them are very agreeable out of office, but adamant in business. They are successful, structured, focused and in control; good businessmen, but what can they build upon in the long run? Employees have come and gone, and those who have stayed have had to keep their voices down. Many have been unhappy in the company of those men.

The Female Leader – The Diplomat

In short, female leadership takes more time. Since female managers more often strive for unity, their decisions are carefully considered before they are made and consequences are analysed. This may sound unfocused but in the long run, when you have a group where the status is clear and you know each other, everything runs smoothly and decisions are made easily and quickly.

But that is a long-term process, and you rarely get that far. We haven't got time. The report must be delivered tomorrow and everywhere there are men with too little to do, needing a consistent flow of reports so they can fill their days and take part in different meetings. Some ten years ago, I interviewed twenty-five women in a project called Wartegg. I found that these women had a more male view on women than most others. They had all had a good relationship with their fathers and had spent much time with them from early age. The twenty-five women had experience of being treated as equals, in other words, as boys. The conclusion is that you learn to handle work life better if you spend time with somebody who knows his way around there, just like in any other area. If you spend your days with a carpenter, you will learn how to craft wood.

Women often tell me that women are the most counteractive sex, working against and reacting in a negative way to each other. I have never run into that in real life, and I believe that it is a tall tale. What I on the other hand *have* experienced is that women who make a career for themselves tend to act like men, in manners as well as language. Anything else would be peculiar. At the companies where I have worked, we have always had a tendency to copy the boss, even when it comes to choosing a necktie in the morning, so it's not strange at all if the women act like the men. You have to use a language that everyone in the group understands.

But the women haven't been less female just because of that; we just think so out of the current standards. They have just been human beings. There are as many tough women as there are awkward and gutless men.

Women keep a distance from their careers and understand that nobody knows what they will be doing in five years. Generally, men talk in terms like: 'In five years, I will… and then I am going to…' Women are much more humble and talk about achievement and joy, 'and perhaps that will lead to my advancing in the company, but you have to see to that you are happy in your private life too.'

That attitude doesn't exist in the male world. As a man, you always accept an offer that involves a fancy title and a raised salary, and after that you try to arrange your personal life. To do otherwise wouldn't be masculine, would it?

On the other hand, men have had no practise when it comes to domestic problems and children. Mummy unpacked your bag when you were twelve and returned home after ice hockey training, didn't she?

The Future Leader

We approach each new era with new demands on leadership. Of course, we have said that for many years, but it's getting serious at last. The oncoming generations won't sit back and let us steer them. They will demand to take part. I'm positive that the new leader style will be in favour of women; there is no place for leadership of the old kind. The new generations have been raised with the privilege of looking elsewhere if they aren't offered personal development and the chance to enjoy activities in their leisure hours. They will raise quite different demands, and maybe they will prefer time with their families to a city jeep. However, it is impossible to foresee what will happen. Of course, it also depends on what will happen to the labour market in general. At present, the western world is experiencing the removal of industrial production to low-salary countries, and that development certainly doesn't support a more equal society. You can foresee harder competition for reduced employment opportunities.

With another recession, the equality debate will disappear and the authoritarian manager will be back in business.

The Directed

There is a close interplay between leaders and those who want to be directed. The latter allow the leader to behave in a certain way, perhaps even an unacceptable way from a social and ethical perspective. Leaders can get away with breaking rules and flouting standards that we are normally so keen that everyone follows. That is a problem for women who want to make a career. The standards are deeply rooted in most people's minds, and we all do our best to prevent changes, not out of evilness, more out of fear for the threat against our own positions. It is also because we find it uncomfortable to have to think in a new way and learn something new.

Our need to belong to a group and to behave like 'everyone else' is one of our major shortcomings. Actually, it's tragic that we don't have the guts to stand up more for our thoughts about right and wrong. That is, of course, a big problem in the business world, especially for the leader. He or she has no idea what the management group really think since the participants act the same way they did in school. They keep quiet, agree, and express their views after the meeting. They suffer from being tongue-tied because of the leader's dominant manners – manners that often remind us of our parents. It seems more important to be popular and share the glory, be awarded privileges and maybe make some extra money that you don't actually deserve at all.

Recruiting High Level Performers

When recruiting new managers and leaders, you always want the best. Absurd quality demands are not unusual. A demand that sometimes appears is that 'in this position, we require a man'. This is usually expressed loudly and clearly, and it can be said without a reaction from anyone. Less common is the demand for a woman. At best, they say that it doesn't matter, i.e. that a woman will do.

To separate the candidates, tests of various kinds are often used. Tests can be projective (pictures), consist of short or long question forms or be logically-analytically oriented. The person with the highest score in the logical tests is considered 'best'. And the tests favour men. They are created to favour men. Created by men for men.

The more sensitive, creative talent – female, perhaps – is in itself much more developmentally oriented. After all, life is about building, not destroying, so it would be desirable if we took better care of people with that kind of talent. You know, you're not just supposed to accommodate and promote yourself, it is just as important to allow other people to develop. Women are good at helping others, much better than men. But they are worse at putting themselves forward. And in a recruiting situation, the winner is the one who presents himself as strong.

Through interviews, tests, references and follow-ups we can get an image of the high-level performers. My description below regarding personality variables builds upon the thousands of interviews I have performed since 1982. These are male standards and designations, and women are bound to lose because they are compared with male advantages defined by men. It's almost akin to when American scientists in the fifties tried to prove that black people were less intelligent than white people. The intelligence tests they used were, as always, developed with white college students and several of the black test subjects could hardly read. The result was obvious: blacks were less intelligent.

High Level Performers' Qualities

1. SELF-CENTRED

The leader likes to place himself in a central position whenever possible. That doesn't mean that the leader always takes command, but he is very present and makes sure that this is noticed. Most leaders are hurt if you don't consider their opinions, and if they don't say anything you'd better make sure that they get an opportunity to comment. It's unfortunate for the forthcoming project if you haven't got the leader with you. If you forget to inform him about what's going on, you've got yourself an enemy – maybe for life.

2. SOCIALLY COMPETENT

The leader has his own opinion on what social intercourse and communication is all about, and it is his idea of the world and his terms that apply. There are many examples of companies where the manager annoys the staff by 'hiding'. He offends many employees by, unconsciously, avoiding greeting them in the morning. He is of course unaware of his strong impact on people around him, both in a positive and a negative sense. Successful people have their own behaviour code, and it's not about snobbery. It's just their image of social competence.

3. HIGH AMBITION LEVEL

The leader's motivation is to reach a higher position, to realise his vision. He wants to win. He accomplishes his assignments as well as he can; the ambition level is high and obvious. That's the motivation, and it has nothing to do with greed. This can change in the long run, but greed is not a part of the basic personality.

4. AVOIDS STRESS

The leader is almost never put under pressure. He experiences his work as his life mission. He mixes work with spare time and family and always makes sure that someone else takes care of the practical details. At home, that person is usually a woman, and she removes the pressure by handling the service tasks.

That's what women are deemed to be best at. Supporting us men, through thick and thin, at work as well as at home. Back home, the women are wives, cleaning-women and mistresses, and at work they are office wives. I have always had one of those, not in a sexual sense, but I have had someone who has handled most of my work and kept an eye on what should be done.

The best way for a man to make a career is to arrange things the way they are back home – to see to that a woman takes care of the heavy and filthy parts of the job. And women who climb really high in their careers also have a helpful husband, domestic help and a nanny.

5. LIVES IN THE PRESENT TIME

The leader is good at isolating incidents and never mixes them with daily activities. He doesn't allow anything other than what's going on at the moment disturb him. The future doesn't scare him; neither do mistakes he has made. He takes one thing at a time and the status anguish is more like a motivation than a drag.

It's natural that your private life has influence on you at work. But since the woman is mainly responsible for the family, the man doesn't have to experience this vulnerability and uneasiness.

6. AGGRESSIVENESS

The aggressiveness is very extrovert and is ever-present. It's extrovert in its energy, and it is obvious. This can appear in the form of outbursts and minor explosions, but also in the form of active silence. This always affects the surroundings in the expected way. It's all about being very obviously present without actually participating.

The more explosive kind of aggressiveness has several different expressions, from dissociation to clear power influence through threats or by sheer energy. Successful men and women have access to their energy and use it in a psychological and physical way so that everyone around is either carried along or abandons the project or the firm just because the pressure becomes unbearable.

The aggressiveness and the energy are strong among successful people and their view on failure is different from most people's. If you fail, it is more like a temporary setback because the rest of the world isn't ready for the kind of idea you introduced. The actor, the artist, the manager and the entrepreneur possess an internal flame and a virtual garden they can visit to look at the complete product.

All of us have an element of aggressiveness inside. The question is how we use it and in what direction we aim it: inwards or outwards, with consideration or misdirectedly aggressive.

Those of us who can use our aggressiveness and energy outwards in a constructive way achieve goals. The others, those who aim this power inwards, become self-accusing and are left behind when the train leaves the platform. They grow more and more intent on pleasing others.

This last sentence implies, from my point of view, what male and female is all about.

7. WORK IS TOP PRIORITY

The leader believes that life is work. Many successful older people – mainly men – habitually express regrets about never having had more time for their families. I doubt that they are sincere when they claim that. Once in their life, they made a deliberate choice and have lived by it ever since. Most of them would have been unhappy if they hadn't been pushed forward by their passion. The urge to succeed, to stand in the limelight, is life to them. That can't be replaced by spending time with the children or in the summer cottage. The wife takes care of the family.

At a board meeting some time ago, the chairman wanted to discuss a matter with me and one of my colleagues. My colleague replied that he couldn't spare the time because he was supposed to do some household shopping before going home. The chairman looked at him and said, quite seriously, 'OK, is your wife ill?'

8. OPINION ON HUMAN NATURE

The careerist looks upon himself as an authority – through his personality or his talents – and has consequently no actual fear of other authorities. However, cooperation problems might arise. Those situations are easily solved by getting rid of the one conflicting entity. The leader prefers to work with somewhat less competent copies of himself, and that is mostly an instinctive process.

The overall outlook is positive, and nothing is really impossible. The stimulation in working with successful people lies in their ability always to see possibilities and the fact that they always have the stamina to work for yet longer when everyone else has left for home.

Even the negative high-level performers have that attitude. They may be pessimists in their view of humanity and they may think that they are surrounded by idiots, but they nevertheless inspire their co-workers and won't let themselves be discouraged. If it appears there is too much dead weight, they fire some employees and hire some new. To this extent, people are regarded as products or merchandise.

Are leaders and managers psychopaths? No, psychopaths are hardly a majority among our leaders. Neither are the absolute black-and-white-thinking people. However, many successful people can choose to see the world divided in to black and white. By acting that way, leaders can easily screen off emotional aspects and enjoy their golf round or hunting session – even after having fired a thousand people or deeply insulting a colleague.

Usually, successful people have one or two confidants with whom they discuss and talk all the time. Other staff members become background figures without influence. Many who work close to a successful semi-celebrity become so dedicated that they become silent, and the leader becomes surrounded by more and more 'yes' men. Among human characteristics there is one attitude that is really destructive: you either agree or keep quiet.

The male leader has a conservative view on women. Mothers have been the symbol for home, food and care. New women take over the service part as successors to the mother. There are lots of stories about great men who consume women – wives, mistresses and prostitutes.

Success

Well, this may seem like a ponderous list. But take it for what it is. Careerists may have several of these 'qualities', but not every one. However, you ought to keep some in your equipment if you want to go all the way to the top.

Success may be a strong word that stands for different qualities for different people. My mother, Astrid Engström, believed it to be a mark of great success that I was the only one of three siblings that went to university. But actually, Astrid Engström was much more successful than I was. It all depends on where you start.

Astrid once worked as a cleaning-woman and sold candy at the movie theatre in Skutskar. But she had a vision of a different life and of being accepted. When she died in 1966, she had advanced within the municipal hierarchy in Alvkarleby and had a position as department manager. That was an impressive climb and a huge success for her and for us, her family.

The concept of success is relative, as with top achievements. It always comes down to what your point of comparison, what your starting point is and what you expect from the person in question. That Susanna Kallur became Swedish champion at 100 metres hurdle is no longer regarded as an achievement, but a few years ago we really thought so. Nowadays we expect her to be best in the world: in some respects she has failed.

My first definition of success is to surpass your own goals and create something that lasts. That's what I believed until I met the writer Patricia Tudor. She turned quite a few of my opinions upside down and said that success is when you can connect interior with exterior.

Tudor means that success must be something more than your achievements. What you work with must harmonise with who you are. When your interior meets with your exterior, you have reached success and can become a whole person – maybe even a 'free' person.

That definition scares me when I regard the world and think about what it looks like out there. How many men with power have that kind of harmony?

In lots of interviews during twenty-five years, I have met a large number of men who claim that their profession was determined by their parents, most often by the father and what he was doing for a living. These men have reached an exterior success but not an interior, and they haven't reached success on their own terms. Could it be that this is the reason to all the frustration, all the cruelty and maltreatment? All the injustices that strike innocent people in working life as well as in the private sphere? There are quite a few distorted brains out there, lots of men who carry out actions that they actually don't want to.

In order to reach and keep positions, women must learn to be more ruthless, to grab opportunities – but who wants that kind of development? The alternative is to reject the quick and easy solutions that appear to save the next quarter of the year. To start looking at leadership with more female eyes.

The question is: who'll start that process? As early as in the mid eighties, these thoughts were brought up. At managerial courses, people talked about how important it is that men learn to develop their feminine qualities – intuition, social competence and sensitivity.

A lot of words, but nothing really happened.

Women – This Is For You

Follow the Male Rules

I believe that women who want to change the balance of power and make a career must accept how things stand at present and follow the rules – men's rules, men's language, men's way of thinking. On the whole, the male power position is strongly anchored in a tradition that goes back several hundred years. The fact that these rules may be, well, stupid and totally based on men's conditions is a reality that we men, and all women, have to deal with.

In order to accomplish a permanent change, women must enter the system and attack the problem from the inside. If there is an increase in the number of women who get access to positions, and especially to top positions, within trade and industry and within the public sector, the bigger will be the chance of a change where new standards can be set that favour both sexes.

I am convinced that the labour market and society can be changed, otherwise I wouldn't have written this book. But you can only change from the inside, through positions of power.

In the Short Run

Personally, I believe that it will be difficult to change present conditions in the short run without legislation. Keeping in mind that changes in behaviour and valuations take time, that is probably the only possibility if we want to see a change in our lifetime.

Women can achieve some goals themselves, and it is possible to change the agenda if you study the rules of the game and stick to them. But that requires women really wanting to bring about changes. I am far from certain that a majority is interested enough to bother about or dare to do that.

Johan Stael von Holstein, a well-known IT entrepreneur in Sweden, once told me how tired he was of women who nagged about how difficult it is to make a breakthrough. If they spent all that energy on doing instead of talking, they would be on their way, he claimed.

When I started to work on this book, I intended to call one of the sectors 'tips' or 'suggestions'. However, I was advised against that by some of the women who read the manuscript. That would be to go too far. Who was I to think that I, a man, could advise women about their behaviour?

I do that anyway, indirectly, because I think I might actually have a few useful tips.

To Act Like a Man

In some situations, women have to act like men to stand a chance. They must talk like men, dress like men and behave like men in different situations.

Much can be said about this, and I am definitely not in favour of preserving the current conditions. 'To act like a man' is in my mind more like a practical standpoint, confirmed by hundreds of women I have interviewed during recruitment situations and coaching.

So, women must learn the rules and follow them. But that also means that women and men must cooperate in this matter if any changes are to be made. However, it all has to be initiated by the women themselves. History knows few cases where one group of people has promoted the freedom of another group and been successful.

The abolition of slavery wasn't carried out by Abraham Lincoln. The rebellion came from within, made its way into American society and finally ceased, at least on the surface.

Competent Women

The number of women who occupy important managerial positions is increasing. That is a fact, yet you still sometimes get a feeling that there are no competent women around. At least, that is what men on the lookout for new talent used to claim. But of course they exist. All you have to do is to scan the right networks.

There are still comparatively few women in top positions, and every time someone is appointed it causes big headlines in the newspapers. The fact that we have a few women in key positions has so far had no heavy impact on women as a group within trade and industry.

For women, much comes down to having the courage to step forward. For companies, it's also a matter of courage: the courage to hire women for top positions.

But, paradoxically, we at the same time experience the phenomenon that female managers in stock-exchange-listed companies are practically non-existent. The possibility for women to influence has increased in companies and organisations, but more often women have indirect power. I know many male managers with female coaches. These women are often titled assistants, secretaries, personnel managers or information managers. They operate in the background even if many within the organisation know how it works. If these women had been men, they would have been top managers.

It is more difficult for women to be acknowledged as managers. One of the reasons is that we have learnt to picture a manager as an older man, big, strong and with authority. During meetings, men always look at each other and the oldest man is addressed, even if there is a younger man or woman at the table. This pattern is followed whether they know who the manager is or not.

Younger women have told me that men seem to find it difficult to look at them, to have eye contact, when there is another man present. You automatically address the man when it comes to making a decision.

Are working days eighteen hours long in management circles? Of course not. That's a lie and it frightens young, ambitious women away from the career road. And I don't believe that you can be a good parent if you are away from home. The whole quality instead of quantity concept is nonsense, just a good old defence mechanism.

I believe that all these factors only strengthen the myths and structure of the male power system and work as an efficient way to prevent women from even thinking about making a career.

Allocation of Quotas and Recruitment

For a couple of years the subject of legislation to clear a path for women to enter the boardrooms has come up from time to time. A national Swedish organisation for trade and industry opposes such a law and claims that competence should be the decisive factor.

Well, well. Does anyone really believe that it is because of competence men occupy seats in boards and managerial groups? Contacts, friendship, personal relations, services in return or sheer chance are rather common reasons, I would say.

Today, there can't be anyone who believes that there are no competent women around. Besides, there are ways to find these women nowadays. Female networks are ubiquitous, so it is just a matter of where to start the search.

But the big issue is rather why women should be on boards at all. Wouldn't it better if they took places in management groups? That way they could influence the values and norms of the company. No boards have any actual influence over recruitment, managership or result. In general, the board knows nothing about what is happening except for the information provided by the general manager. Isn't that right?

The board can be of great symbolic value, of course: for the students at the university, for women and employees and for the image of the company. So women should of course make their way into boards as well as management groups.

I haven't heard any woman, apart from some politicians, who supports the demand for legislation. There can be different reasons for that. You agree but keep quiet, or you simply consider it unimportant whether there are more women in the boardrooms.

As an example, I can mention that more than 90% of the members in Ruter Dam, a Swedish network for female managers, said a flat 'no' to legislation. Anyone who has worked within trade and industry, and I believe it is the same within the federal or municipal world, knows that in order to influence structures you have to be in a management group. I don't know of any company that I have worked with during recent years in which there has been discussion about the constitution of the board. Or discussions about female issues.

So why allocate quotas? All you have to do is elect the most suitable people. There is no evidence that women are outnumbered in this respect. It is the current recruitment policies that have to be changed.

It goes without saying that men do recruit men to boards and all other positions. In all forms of recruiting, it is much easier to talk to and identify yourself to someone of your own kind. Men believe that they know how other men work, but it is debatable whether they know anything about women. Apart from, that is, what they learned during their first ten to twelve years.

Rights and Goals

There are some easy questions you can ask yourself:

- Where do you want to go?
- What are you prepared to do to get there?
- What resources are required?
- How are you going to act in order to reach your goal?

In general, men find it easier to recognise their rights and defend them. In fact, they mostly take them for granted. We know that this is due to upbringing and structures of society. Perhaps it is time for you to consider the following:

- Why don't you allow yourself the right which you accept that others are entitled to?
- Is there something in your past that makes you believe you don't have that right?
- What would happen if you allowed yourself that right?

People who have taken advantage of you in the past won't always react in a positive way when you suddenly act independently and start to care for yourself. There are many examples of what happens when women rise and claim their right to develop their talents. You can count on being counteracted as soon as you pronounce the word 'equality'. But if you believe in your rights, you understand why you have to keep fighting even if you aren't encouraged by others.

Pitfalls in Conversations

Conversations are very important in a person's life. We all want to be understood, seen and acknowledged. However, the conditions of communication are different for men and women.

Ever since he was a little boy, the man has been used to making his voice heard and being taken seriously. A man is allowed to have a strong presence and he takes it for granted that he is listened to. For girls and women it is different. Most of them have never been trained or encouraged, kindergarten, school or at home, to speak up and make their presence felt. We men have been taught that if women are given their say, we will have to put up with too-long and too-emotional monologues.

The problem for most women is that they believe that men are as interested as they are in letting all parties have their say and meeting each other on an adult level. However, men are seldom interested in that, perhaps due to lack of training and understanding. Men want to get things done and move on. This is how disconnected we have become from the process of socialising. Don't believe the myth about the caveman. It's only a lot of rubbish that reinforces the prejudice.

The conversation during an interview is unnatural since it is tailored to a very unequal relationship. For the person being interviewed it is important to give the right impression and to give the answers you believe are expected to tricky questions.

For women, a number of pitfalls may occur during conversations with men, not least during interviews. From the woman's point of view, she expects to meet a serious person who is there to do a professional job. My experience tells me that this is unfortunately not always the case – not initially, anyway. If you, as a woman, want to be successful during a conversation or during an interview, you have to be aware of the male game rules.

Show Who You Are

Let us in the following examples suppose that the person who is being interviewed is a woman and the recruiter is a man.

The first thing you can assume, without generalising or being prejudiced, is that he has prejudices about women. Regardless of whether the man is young or old, he has a distorted image of women. It's your responsibility to make sure that you talk about and mean the same thing. It's all about making yourself understood. He pictures his mother or wife in front of him and believes that he knows what women in general are like. Your most important task will be to make him understand that you are an individual, not someone who represents womankind.

You also have to hold on to your own image of yourself in order not to let the recruiter give you a role that suits his employer's purpose.

Disturbing Thoughts

It is rather common that during the first minutes of the conversation the male recruiter, or for that matter the manager or his colleague, is thinking about you and sex. He is wondering whether he can get you into bed or not, or about the size of your breasts. I have never met a man who doesn't recognise himself or other men in that description. It influences, of course, all kinds of conversations and not least a process of recruitment. Wherever I have been working, men have always made comments about women's looks. Anna Wahl, a researcher at the university of economics and business administration in Stockholm, the capital of Sweden, has in several of her books shown that the interplay between men and women often has a sexual tension. In a couple of books she shows that meetings between men and women always have many concealed agendas. There are often latent motives, difficult to pinpoint if you are unaware of the rules.

Never Hesitate

For a woman, it is especially important to think about what kind of language you use. To say 'I have never tried that' or 'perhaps I could do that after some practise' doesn't show that you are a humble, reflective and smart person, if that's what you think. It only shows a timid, insecure person, unable to make her own decisions and unfit to be a leader. If you say that you don't want to make decisions and that you don't want to take risks, you only demonstrate lack of ambition. Recruiters are looking for ambitious people, willing to go for it.

Pay Attention to Tests

Recruiters use tests for their guidance. Beware of them!

You are of course in an awkward position, but you have the right to say no, and that shouldn't have any impact on your chances. If you do go through a test, you have the right to know the result, no matter what the recruiter says. Anyone can handle tests and anyone can read the results and talk them over with you. Most recruiters use tests to silence their own insecurity, to get the better of the situation and, not the least, to get handsomely paid.

So, demand your right to look at the result of the test and what the American computer programme has to say about you. It's all about your life and your future. No matter what they say, the results of the test are saved for a period of time and the recruiter's client has access to part of it. At worst, a complete copy is handed over as well.

The purpose of the test is not that you shall be able to recognise yourself. The purpose is to find out if you are the right person for a certain position in a certain company. So if the recruiter manages to correctly identify your personality, don't let that impress you. That is not due to the test but to the conversation you have had with him.

Dress Code

When you go to important meetings, dress up but don't overdo it. Trousers and a jacket. Dark (male) colours. Definitely not in red, save that for the day when you've got the job. It should be simple, tidy and expensive. Black or grey.

Difficult to Change

I am not saying that any of the actions and reactions above is on a conscious level. It's just the way it works, and it's tough to change the pattern. The younger generation of recruiters learn from the older and take on their prejudices. We must start from when children are small if we want to change focus on gender roles.

I can be very pessimistic when I think about this and wonder if it will be the same when my grandchildren take over. I hope I will be proven wrong. Changes are nasty, frightening and dangerous. We all know that, and we fight to stick with what we have. It takes some guts for a recruiter to choose a woman before a man.

There are few occasions when I or any colleague that I know of have recommended a woman unless it's been within an area believed to be better suited to a woman, such as the service sector. I am ashamed to admit this, but I have never thought about it this way before. You might think that I have spent most of my professional life in male-dominated environments, but that is not true. It has rather been the opposite, since there always have been many women in the recruitment business.

Not until the past few years has this issue been seriously discussed, by either sex. But we seem to be heading in the right direction, as the question is raised more often and with greater emphasis.

Summary

Based on my interviews, I have made the following summary:

- Be straight and clear and never speak derogatorily about yourself or your work.

- Let zest and joy be your prime motivation.

- Strive to see possibilities and find solutions.

- Always have the overall result in sight. Make sure that the whole team aim at the same target.

- Broaden your competence.

- Always be alert.

- Make yourself visible and don't hesitate to be the one who makes the decisions.

- Don't let yourself be interrupted. Demand to be taken seriously and that people around you listen to what you have to say.

- Keep in mind that intuition and emotions don't impress men. They doubt the existence of body language.

- Don't work too much. It's a myth, nothing but an empty threat, that people in managerial positions work eighteen hours a day.

- Create your own position in the office and make clear to the company how much money they will earn through this.

- Always be on time or rather five minutes ahead. This will give you a mental advantage.

- Find yourself a male mentor to teach you the company language and the rules of the game.

- Go your own way. Find your personal style to act and work.

- Don't believe that the men know more than you do. They take chances and so should you!

- Choose the right life partner. Live in an equal relationship.

- Remind yourself that you are a role model in your position and have an ethical responsibility.

To the Management Group

Equality Initiatives of the Organisation

All companies and organisations can get on with the equality work without delay. My suggestion is that you as a manager start with briefings with your staff. Be honest and say that this issue has up to now been neglected but that it will henceforth be an important item on the agenda. You clarify the current work of equality and the plans for the next two years.

Show the timetable and what measures the company aims to take. Be clear to point out that all changes are valid from now on. There's no reason to wait. This is about human rights and they are laid down by law.

Anyone who doesn't comprehend what it's all about or shows no understanding of why it's necessary should be asked to leave the company.

Concrete Measures

Introduce the people who will lead the whole equality project. One of them should be recruited from the managerial group and it has to be a man. Let the men settle the injustices they have, for so long, neglected to do anything about. The consequences for the company will be increased respect and increased profit. Even the medial attention will increase.

These are the concrete measures you as manager ought to force through:

1. Make sure that the company or organisation has as many female as male managers, on all levels. Initiate an external and internal recruitment programme and look for female candidates only.

2. Put a man in charge of all projects regarding equality work. Employ a young marketing officer who understands what the whole thing is about.

3. Introduce penalties for sexual harassment. Fire the oppressors. That goes for any form of harassment, of course.

4. Cancel pay talks with heads of departments if they can't show an equality balance in their departments. Ask employees anonymously how they feel about the situation before having pay talks or discussions of development with your subordinate directors.

5. Make sure that issues of equality have a fixed position on the agenda during management meetings. This item shall be of the same importance as sales figures.

6. Stop making remarks about women and their bodies even behind what you think are closed doors. There is no such thing and everything you say as a manager will be the norm of the company or organisation. Remember to be a good role model.

7. Hire women when you engage business development consultants. They have broader experience than young and expensive male consultants.

8. Freeze the wages for all men five years forward, or until the wages of women have reached the same level. Nothing but the same wages for the same kind of work is acceptable.

9. Make it compulsory to report violations of the code. Anyone who hears or sees that someone is being harassed without reporting it is to be considered an accessory.

Interviews

Before I started writing this book, I met and talked to thirty women. Here are some of the stories that came out of these conversations.

An obvious list of how to act as a manager and leader came from Anna Björklund, general manager of Pengar i Sverige, a company which is owned by Securitas and has ridden out a few storms.

Anna Björklund claims that you have to 'wrap yourself,' – meaning that you should be extremely clear about your message. Important considerations are how you talk, how you move and how you look. Her list is rather simple: 'Wrap yourself, don't talk too much, use plain terms. When you talk at a meeting, stand up, look the person you are addressing right in the eyes, use a firm voice and don't be afraid of confrontations.'

Anna Björklund practises what she preaches; she answers my questions in plain terms. Regarding feminine and masculine styles, she says that women must understand that 'some decisions are not democratic'. She claims there are a lot of competent women, 'it just depends on in which network you are searching'. Her opinion is that the allocation of quotas debate is necessary, but not legislation. The debate itself has certainly been more effective than a law would be.

Anna Björklund regards work as a part of life. She thinks it's important to work with meaningful tasks and to succeed in changing matters. She thinks that her husband is 'special' as he has always looked upon home and children as something to be shared equally. In her opinion, men in general consider women stupid, and unfortunately many women buy this. Women are subordinate in social structures, and the efforts to change that are in progress, according to Anna Björklund.

Victoria Strand is the general manager of a subsidiary company within Ericsson. She considers it important to gain a broad competence before being appointed as a manager.

Having graduated as an engineer, she has later worked as a manager within the fields of personnel and information. Her spontaneous list starts with her choice of husband. Not without a glint in her eye, she says that 'A woman who wants to make a career must have the right kind of husband. You can't succeed if you're the only one in the household with two jobs. A broad competence and a dig-where-you-are philosophy will lead new challenges your way.

'But they won't come by themselves. You need to make the right decisions, of course, but you must also let people know that you are good.

'A mentor is priceless. To have an older and more experienced person to rely on means that you can eliminate the worst blunders and that you have someone who gives you feedback and who is not influenced by relations and history of the company.'

Victoria Strand is a cheerful person who laughs a lot and doesn't take life too seriously. There's a joyous sphere around her and our conversation is far from what it would have been like with a male general manager at Ericsson.

Annika Dopping, an author and journalist, sparkles with joy. In everything she's engaged in, she has a strong dedication. She thanks her twin brother for 'teaching me to control the room'. You have to take command.

Like many of the other women I have met, she talks about the fun and joy in working. It is important to have a mission, to look for experiences and to spread small treasures around you. In short, if you share you will receive. She believes that many women slip through the system because they don't understand the cultural differences and the pecking order. Some women miss that and never realise what can be interpreted as hostile.

If you don't know the rules and overstep your authority, you won't be taken seriously. Maybe you'll even be impeded. Annika believes that the motivation of the ego is vital if you wish to accomplish changes and improvements.

She suggests that democracy sometimes must be put aside. There are questions and matters that have to be dealt with now, at this moment, and there isn't time for a discussion or a voting. And she believes that women more than men interpret that as being run over.

Madeleine Onne has throughout her life been connected to the Royal Opera in Stockholm. Her career was crowned when she became a Prima Ballerina and to top that she was also appointed head of the Royal Ballet in 2002.

Just like Annika Dopping, she talks about the powers within you, and her dedication sends vibrations through the room. Her energy glitters and she always needs something to keep her occupied.

Madeleine says that you must use your own stamina and make things happen. No one will help you for nothing, you rule over your own career. Her energy is so vivid she watches TV with a computer on her lap; there is always some job to finish.

Now she has an appointment over three years and regards that as a big challenge. There is no doubt in her mind about succeeding and the basis of her leadership is that everyone will join her in her pursuit.

Margareta Norell works at the Swedish Royal Technical Academy as a professor of integrated product development within techniques and organisation. She is also a Vice President. Margareta believes that women must create platforms of their own and from there see which way to go. In other words, to try to take command of your own career. Initially, she gives an almost shy impression, but after a while her iron will and inexhaustible energy become obvious. Margareta has worked hard for a long time, 'more than I can tell people', and in this way she reminds me of many women I have met. Working capacity is often a determining factor – to have the strength to stay when everyone else goes home. Margareta sets new goals before the old ones are fulfilled; you have to be on your toes all the time. She doesn't feel that she has met that much resistance, but in some organisations and companies she has sometimes noticed that an old-boy attitude increases when you reach higher levels in the hierarchy.

Patricia Tudor-Sandahl, an author and psychotherapist, has written in a number of books about the importance of 'the interior and the exterior matching'. In short, that you work with what you wish to do and enjoy.

But can everyone really do that? We all have a responsibility for what we do, and if you don't want to just float along, you have to accept your responsibility.

Patricia believes that the motivation is to live in the present and to combine that with discipline. You must allow yourself to be committed to the moment to accomplish anything genuine. She thinks that you can be successful just on your own terms, but you can also be forced into something and must choose between taking or rejecting the challenge. You always have a choice. So what have you got to lose from trying to do your best?

According to Patricia, success is not worth any price. There must be an element of ethics in the whole thing. You have a responsibility, because when you are successful, you are an example for many others.

My Conclusions

Above all, it has been very obvious to me that many female managers have a certain detachment towards themselves. They don't believe that the world revolves around them and them alone.

That doesn't mean that women take their jobs less seriously. They just have a capacity to watch themselves from above, or perhaps from the side. When you can regard yourself and how you affect your surroundings, you have a better understanding of the shortcomings of others. You simply become a better manager and leader.

Women believe that work shall be important and significant. They wish to work with tasks that have potential for the development of society and people. Doesn't everybody? No. Many men don't even consider that idea. Many men work with destructive projects, from arms and tobacco to drugs and trafficking, and think nothing about it.

Women can and wish to compete, but they lack the destructive mind of men. To women, winning doesn't automatically mean that there are losers in the race. If someone else was better, well, good for her, but now I'll move on.

Men look down on losers, and from such a position it is difficult to go forward. The destructive male way of regarding other people is strengthened all the time, and I look upon myself just the way I look upon others. And who wants to fail? Who wants to be a loser? Remember the old American proverb: To keep a man down, you have to stay down yourself.

Women have better working capacity than men. Much better, there is no doubt about that. Most women have double working shifts, at work and at home. The higher you reach in the hierarchy, the more help you provide. But you still have the main responsibility.

Many of the women I have met accept that men are

inadequate and that they, being women, must live with a greater
amount of responsibility. Women are less inclined to end up in
the loneliness trap because they believe that they have achieved
something together with others. Men may claim the same, but in
their own minds most men think that they have accomplished
and run a project by themselves. Which, of course, results in their
being unable to comprehend how the company will survive the
day they quit. They are in for a surprise that may last for many
years. Women, on the other hand, may very well themselves raise
the question of their successor.

A Few Final Words

Here I am today. Working with this book has changed me in several ways. I can no longer walk on by, cover my ears or behave as if nothing were the matter when I hear and see how some men act towards women. Every day, things happen and words are spoken that are significant and influence us and our children. Of course, if I decided to react to everything I wouldn't have time for anything else. And there are, naturally, situations where people flirt or make jokes. But if you just know what it's all about, there's usually no problem.

Someone asked me what I feel like now that I have written the book and it is about to be published. Automatically, I answered 'guilty'. Not because I wrote the book but because I woke up so late. So I'll feel good if I 'through this book' can confirm some of the emotions that women have sensed and formulated for many years.

In the future, equality will be on the agenda at every conference and seminar I hold – as a basis component, not as an odd training session. Many companies carry through equality seminars as if they have discovered something new to introduce. It's better to make the whole issue a topic of conversation everywhere, from the boardroom to the cafeteria.

I'm not a feminist, never will be. It's not that I don't want to be, but because I am too indoctrinated to be able to think in any way other than I always have. My mother rotates in her grave when she regards my efforts.

Those who know me say that I have already changed for the better and it couldn't be otherwise. If men read about and discussed this issue, the equality revolution would take much less time and we all would live in a better society.

I'm in the middle of a process that is turning me into a more complete person and I can observe the interplay between women and men in a totally new way. And I promise you, fellows, it's much more exciting than you know.

The last two years I have been travelling around Sweden, talking at seminars and working with management teams and managers. Sweden has a long way to go before we can say that there is equality between men and women. Swedes may say that we have come a long way, but most of it is on the surface. We have a lot of work still to do. So let's get started.